LESSONS FROM VERNACULAR ARCHITECTURE

The architectural community has had a strong and continuing interest in traditional and vernacular architecture. This has been rekindled by the need to develop an architecture that works with climate, rather than against it, to create more sustainable buildings. Most earlier research and existing publications on traditional or vernacular architecture have followed an anthropological or archaeological approach, whereas books on climatic design and sustainable architecture tend to refer to contemporary principles and built precedents without direct reference to past experience.

Lessons from Vernacular Architecture takes lessons directly from traditional and vernacular architecture and offers them to the reader as guidance and inspiration for new buildings. The appropriate technical and social solutions provided by vernacular and traditional architecture are analysed in detail. International case studies focus on environmental design aspects of traditional architecture in a broad range of climatic conditions and building types.

Willi Weber is an architect and Professor of Building Physics at the Institute of Environmental Sciences of the University of Geneva, Switzerland. As director of the University's Centre for the Study of Energy Problems (CUEPE) he was in charge of a research group involved in expert appraisals in the field of energy and environment in architecture. He was the chairman of the 23rd International PLEA (Passive and Low Energy Architecture) Conference that was held in Geneva in 2006.

Simos Yannas is the Director of the Environment & Energy Studies Programme at the Architectural Association School of Architecture in London, UK where he is responsible for the Masters programmes in Sustainable Environmental Design and the AA School's PhD Programme. His previous book with Earthscan, *Roof Cooling Techniques: a Design Handbook* (2005), was shortlisted for the Royal Institute of British Architects' RIBA Bookshops International Book Award in Architecture. He is a founding member of the PLEA international network.

LESSONS FROM VERNACULAR ARCHITECTURE

Edited by Willi Weber and Simos Yannas

Routledge
Taylor & Francis Group
LONDON AND NEW YORK

earthscan
from Routledge

First published 2014
by Routledge
2 Park Square, Milton Park, Abingdon, Oxon, OX14 4RN

Simultaneously published in the USA and Canada
by Routledge
711 Third Avenue, New York, NY 10017

Routledge is an imprint of the Taylor & Francis Group, an informa business

British Library Cataloguing in Publication Data
A catalogue record for this book is available from the British Library

Library of Congress Cataloging-in-Publication Data
Lessons from vernacular architecture/edited by Willi Weber and
Simos Yannas.
    pages cm
    Includes bibliographical references and index.
    1. Sustainable architecture. 2. Vernacular architecture.
    I. Weber, Willi, editor of compilation. II. Yannas, Simos,
    editor of compilation.
    NA2542.36.L47 2013
    720.9—dc23   2013000367

ISBN13: 978–1–84407–600–0 (hbk)
ISBN13: 978–0–203–75616–4 (ebk)

Typeset in Bembo and Stone Sans
by Florence Production Ltd, Stoodleigh, Devon, UK

Printed in Great Britain by Bell & Bain Ltd, Glasgow

CONTENTS

ILLUSTRATIONS

Figures

Maps

Graphs

Tables

CONTRIBUTORS

Riccardo Balbo is a Lecturer in Digital Architectural Design at the School of Built Environment, University of Salford, UK and Visiting Professor in Architecture at the Politecnico di Torino, Italy. His paper here is based on a research project sponsored by the Italian government within the framework of scientific and technical co-operation between Italy and Egypt.

Jean Bouillot worked as an architect in the Middle East and West Africa for over fifteen years before setting up practice in Beaune, France embracing the principles of bioclimatic design and undertaking projects locally as well as around the Mediterranean and in Jordan and China.

José María Cabeza-Lainez is Professor of Architecture at the University of Seville, Spain. A graduate in oriental studies, he is fluent in many languages, including Japanese and Chinese. He is a Research Fellow at the Universities of Hokkaido and Kobe Design, a member of the Spanish Research Council's scientific committee on Asia and the Pacific and a Fellow of the Academy of Fine Arts of Seville. Since 2008 he serves as Honorary Consul of Japan in Andalucía.

Anibal Figueroa is Professor of Architecture at the Universidad Autonoma Metropolitana in Mexico and a Member of the National Research Council. His interest in Luis Barragán, since his first meeting with the architect some thirty years ago, has produced numerous articles and two books. **Gloria Castorena** is leading the research group in bioclimatic architecture at the same university.

Joy-Anne Fleming studied architecture at Dundee University and was the first recipient of the Eden Scholarship at the Architectural Association Graduate School, London. Her paper here is based on her Masters dissertation, which focused on the design of a low energy house for rural Northern Ireland inspired by the vernacular Irish cottage. She is currently in practice with Canaway Fleming in London.

Brian Ford is Professor of Bioclimatic Architecture at the School of the Built Environment, University of Nottingham, UK. An architect and environmental design consultant, he has previously studied the environmental performance characteristics of Mughal and pre-Mughal buildings in North India. **Benson Lau** is an architect and environmental design consultant, and currently course director for the MArch in Environmental Design at the School of the Built Environment, University of Nottingham. He has previously studied and published work on the poetics of light in Le Corbusier's religious buildings and has written on the environmental performance of vernacular architecture in China. **Zhang Hongru** is with the Shanghai Research Institute of Building Sciences, China.

Saadet Armağan Güleç, Fatih Canan and **Mustafa Korumaz** are architects undertaking research on sustainable architecture and the restoration of historical buildings at the Department of Architecture, Selcuk University, Turkey.

Amanda Heal, Wayne Forster and **Caroline Paradise** are members of the Design Research Unit at the Welsh School of Architecture, Cardiff, UK, undertaking projects with a particular interest in sustainability, tectonics, material innovation and sensitive landscapes.

Kimberly Kramer is currently a Lecturer in the Faculty of Architecture at Chiang Mai University, Thailand. Her research focuses on vernacular architecture and social responsibility in architecture.

Kevin McCartney is the Director of the Cork Centre for Architectural Education in Ireland. He was previously Director of Research at the School of Architecture in Portsmouth, UK. **Paruj Antarikananda** is an architect working in Thailand. His Masters thesis at the University of Portsmouth generated the empirical data and illustrations that appear in the paper comparing contemporary and traditional houses in Thailand. **Elena Douvlou** is a Senior Lecturer at the School of Architecture, University of Portsmouth, UK.

Habib Melki is Acting Dean of the Faculty of Architecture Art & Design at Notre Dame University, Lebanon. He was the Chairman of the 22nd International PLEA Conference hosted by Notre Dame University in 2005.

Leticia Neves studied architecture at the University of São Paulo, Brazil and completed a Masters thesis on the work of the architect Severiano Porto.

Magda Sibley is a senior lecturer in architecture at the University of Liverpool. She has studied the urban form and architecture of world heritage Islamic cities in North Africa and the Middle East with the aim of informing new design projects. She has co-edited *Courtyard Housing: Past, Present and Future* published in 2006 by Taylor & Francis and participated in the European HAMMAM project.

Thanos N. Stasinopoulos is a freelance architect, researcher and lecturer in green architecture at the National Technical University of Athens and other schools of architecture.

Willi Weber is an architect and Professor of Building Physics at the Institute of Environmental Sciences of the University of Geneva. As director of the University's Centre for the Study of Energy Problems (CUEPE) he was in charge of a research group involved in expert appraisals in the field of energy and environment in architecture. He was the chairman of the 23rd International PLEA Conference that was held in Geneva in 2006.

Simos Yannas is the Director of the Environment & Energy Studies Programme at the Architectural Association School of Architecture in London, UK, where he is responsible for the Masters programmes in Sustainable Environmental Design and the AA School's PhD Programme. His previous book with Earthscan, *Roof Cooling Techniques: a Design Handbook*, was shortlisted for the Royal Institute of British Architects RIBA Bookshops International Book Award in Architecture. He is a founding member of the PLEA (Passive and Low Energy Architecture) international network.

INTRODUCTION

Willi Weber and Simos Yannas

> *... la tradition est la chaîne ininterrompue de toutes les novations et, par delà, le témoin le plus sûr de la projection vers l'avenir.*[1]
>
> (Le Corbusier, 1957, p.144)

The object of this book is to look at one of the most quoted, but least well studied, characteristics of vernacular architecture: its physical relationship with climate and site. Generalized observations on the climatic adaptation of vernacular buildings are plentiful, but detailed and reliable measurements are quite scarce. Discussing the role of climate in *House Form and Culture* Amos Rapoport paid tribute to:

> the amazing skill shown by primitive and peasant builders in dealing with climatic problems, and their ability to use minimum resources for maximum comfort.
>
> (Rapoport, 1969, p.83)

However, the precise role and importance of climate as generative principle for built form is still an open question. Rapoport was careful to lay aside claims of climatic determinism:

> One need not deny the importance of climate to question its determining role in the creation of built form. Examination of the extreme differences in urban pattern and house types . . . shows them to be much more related to culture than to climate.
>
> (Rapoport, 1969, p.19)

Studies of vernacular buildings and settlements conducted since the publication of Rapoport's seminal book corroborate his observations. However, while the built form and materiality of vernacular buildings may suggest their climatic provenance, in itself this is hardly proof of all-year environmental performance. For example, thick masonry construction with small windows, a characteristic of Mediterranean vernacular, can provide daytime indoor temperatures cooler than outdoors on these two features alone, thus serving such buildings well in the hot and sunny summers of this climatic region.[2] In winter, however, with mean daily outdoor temperature hovering around 10–12°C, the small windows and thick masonry walls are at a disadvantage as they jointly prevent indoor temperatures from rising much above these values, which are well below thermal comfort range; the building is thus no longer capable of being free-running and becomes dependent on the hearth and on non-renewable energy sources.

Our objective today is to achieve acceptable indoor environmental conditions for occupants with the least expenditure in energy and materials, replacing non-renewable energy sources with renewable ones and doing away with environmentally unfriendly processes and materials. We have the knowledge of building physics, wide choice in materials that can provide appropriate environmental properties, and a good understanding of what drives environmental performance derived from measurements and simulation studies. What lessons can vernacular architecture continue to hold for us today?

The papers in this book show that there are two important ways in which vernacular architecture continues to be of direct and practical interest for architects and students of architecture today. First, it provides a large pool of buildings on which to study the application of passive techniques of environmental design[3] that are not just technical applications but integral constituents of the buildings' architecture and the inhabitants' lifestyle.

In contrast, few contemporary buildings lend themselves to such study, a situation that is particularly acute in developing countries and warm climates where conventional air conditioning is seen as a panacea and applied indiscriminately.

The second important reason for which vernacular architecture continues to be of direct and practical interest today echoes Le Corbusier's statement at the start of this introduction. Vernacular architecture never ceases to appeal to architects and students of architecture. In this capacity it has often inspired the development of new ideas and projects, acting as a springboard and model for innovation rather than imitation.

The fourteen papers that follow in this book were selected from a larger number presented at the 23rd PLEA Conference held in Geneva on the topic of 'Clever Design, Affordable Comfort'.[4]

Part I of the book highlights different facets and constituents of vernacular architecture as objects of environmental design research. Each chapter is an individual case study on the relationship of the built form with its setting, encompassing the scales of settlement and individual building as well as that of building elements and their components. The treatment of transitions between these different scales and the nature of adaptive opportunities available to inhabitants to modify environmental conditions are of particular interest. Thanos Stasinopoulos, in his essay on the island of Santorini (Chapter 1), identifies the scarce resources and harsh natural setting of the island as the origins of the distinctive architectural language and environmental features of the island's settlements. He argues that on Santorini, functionality and environmental performance were underpinned by the convivial nature of the urban tissue and the communal spirit of the inhabitants. Communal spirit and respect for neighbours' rights to light, fresh air and privacy are recurrent themes in the following paper (Chapter 2), in which Riccardo Balbo – whose research team studied two mud brick settlements at the Dakhleh Oasis in Egypt – finds the strong influence of cultural, social and religious values matched by knowledge of climate and concern for material resources. Focusing on the interface between public and private, the paper traces the guidelines that had shaped the form of the settlements and provided its builders with rules of thumb on the width of streets, the heights of buildings, the position and size of openings and the design of outdoor and semi-outdoor spaces.

On far too many contemporary buildings the indiscriminate orientation, sizing and detailing of windows, combined with poor thermal properties and lack of solar protection, has turned this most potent and multifunctional building element into a major environmental handicap. This is in stark contrast with the care with which windows are treated by vernacular builders. Habib Melki's account of the influences that shaped the evolution of the window in Lebanese vernacular architecture shows how cultural, functional and environmental considerations combined to produce a broad typology of window forms and features that provided formal diversity as well as performative subtlety (Chapter 3).

The next two papers deal with the hammām, a uniquely communal building type that houses distinctly different indoor microclimates. Magda Sibley draws on her surveys of historic public baths in Fez and Damascus to highlight the distinctive characteristics and evolution of this building type (Chapter 4). Of particular interest here is how the built form contributes to the creation and maintenance of its distinct indoor microclimates through the zoning and buffering of spaces and by the coupling of the building to the urban tissue, which results in reduced exposure to the outside while access to natural light and ventilation air is provided by roof apertures. Jean Bouillot reports on a field study and spot measurements at the hammām Bab El Bahr in Cairo, sharing his hypotheses about how the section, internal layout and detailing of the building contribute to its performance (Chapter 5). Unlike the blind external elevations of hammāms, designed to minimize exposure to the outdoor climate, the external envelope of the building described by Brian Ford, Benson Lau and Zhang Hongru (Chapter 6), was clearly intended to be permeable, and the nature of its built form, designed as a succession of pavilions and courtyards, maximizes exposure to the outdoor environment. The paper shows how this design strategy allowed the building to achieve comfortable conditions throughout the year while providing a visually stimulating sequence of spaces.

Transitional spaces such as patios, courtyards, verandas and their many variants are among the most recognizable and environmentally potent features of vernacular architecture. In the last paper of this part of the book Saadet Armağan Güleç, Fatih Canan and Mustafa Korumaz discuss several variants of such spaces as encountered in the traditional settlements of southeast Turkey (Chapter 7). The authors underline the social character, functionality and positive environmental attributes of these traditional features in contrast to their contemporary variants.

Part II of the book is also in the form of a series of case studies. However, here the object of research is not the vernacular in itself, but the way in which engagement with it has inspired subsequent generations of builders, architects and students into new ventures and designs for which vernacular architecture provides a reference or yardstick. Kimberly Kramer's essay on the bungalow (Chapter 8) traces the origins of this dwelling type in the vernacular traditions of India, from where it was developed to provide accommodation for early colonial settlers. While the concepts borrowed from the vernacular were well adapted to the warm climates of the subcontinent they remained at odds with occupants' persistence in maintaining their northern European dress codes and behavioural patterns. Achieving thermal comfort in hot periods required the services of energetic servants in the role now played by mechanical air conditioning. Refined over the years, the bungalow was reproduced across India and eventually exported to Britain and North America. In his homage to Japanese traditional architecture José María Cabeza-Lainez (Chapter 9) focuses on the influence its treatment of daylight and sunlight had on distinguished Western architects such as Bruno Taut and Antonin Raymond, while continuing to inform contemporary Japanese architects and artists. Discussing the bioclimatic attributes in the work of the Mexican architect Luis Barragán, Anibal Figueroa and Gloria Castorena (Chapter 10) argue that Barragán's intuitive and empirical approach was rooted in the methods of vernacular architecture, which gave his work a timeless yet contemporary feel. Leticia Neves' essay (Chapter 11) celebrates the work of Severiano Porto, an architect who, having moved to the Amazon region in the 1970s, adopted local traditional methods, adapted his buildings to climate and site and developed new construction methods making the use of local timber widely acceptable.

Comparison of the thermal performance of the traditional Thai house with one of contemporary design is the topic of the critical essay by Kevin McCartney, Paruj Antarikananda and Elena Douvlou (Chapter 12). Undertaken by computer simulation, the comparison allows the authors close control over the modelling of climatic variables and building design parameters. Given the nature of the country's climates, differences in thermal performance arise primarily from variations in the size and degree of solar protection of windows and to a lesser extent from the thermal capacity of the building structure. Joy-Anne Fleming's design for a 'Wee Energy House' in rural Northern Ireland (Chapter 13) draws inspiration from the traditional cottage form of the region. While maintaining an aesthetic link with local tradition, the design takes advantage of contemporary passive techniques to achieve good comfortable conditions on low running costs. Here thermal simulation studies have helped decide the values of key design parameters optimizing thermal performance.

In the final paper of Part II, Wayne Forster, Amanda Heal and Caroline Paradise (Chapter 14) describe a taught course for first-year architecture students in which study of vernacular buildings at a Welsh open-air museum has provided an experience-based learning context in which the physical characteristics and environmental performance of the buildings are introduced by direct observation and the lessons learnt are immediately applied by the students on their own designs.

In contrast to the teachings of many environmental design textbooks whose message is to minimize this, maximize that, or optimize the other, the main lesson of vernacular architecture is to harmonize, and it is by harmonizing conflicting design requirements that it achieves its sense of community and timelessness. We hope that readers may be encouraged by this book to pursue case studies of their own, drawing from the vernacular traditions of their region on the way to developing new models and prototypes for the present and the future. We will be pleased to hear of any such efforts.

Willi Weber, willi.weber@archiwatt.ch
Simos Yannas, simos@aaschool.ac.uk

Notes

1   '. . . tradition is the unbroken chain of all renewals and, beyond that, the surest witness of the projection toward the future'.
2   The thermal capacity of the thick masonry walls modulates the indoor temperature towards the daily average of the outdoor temperature while small windows limit heat gains from the outside. In this way indoor temperatures can remain below 30°C while the outdoor air temperature rises above 35°C and may feel much warmer for subjects exposed to direct sunshine. At night, when the outdoor temperature falls to the vicinity of 20°C, opening the windows allows daytime heat gains from occupancy to be dissipated and the building can then start the following day at a temperature close to the cool morning temperature outdoors.

3   In contemporary terminology we refer to such design strategies as *passive*, or preferably as *bioclimatic*, to indicate that the mechanisms involved do not depend on mechanical systems but on biological and climatic processes.
4   PLEA stands for Passive and Low Energy Architecture, an international network of experts committed to the development, documentation and diffusion of the principles and practice of *sustainable environmental design*. Since its beginnings in 1981, PLEA has held international conferences in many different countries and climatic regions to study these practices locally and to disseminate them globally.

References

Le Corbusier (1957) 'Entretien avec les étudiants des Ecoles d'Architecture', in *La Charte d'Athènes*, Paris, Ed.de Minuit.
Rapoport, A. (1969) *House form and culture*, Englewood Cliffs NJ, Prentice Hall, Inc.

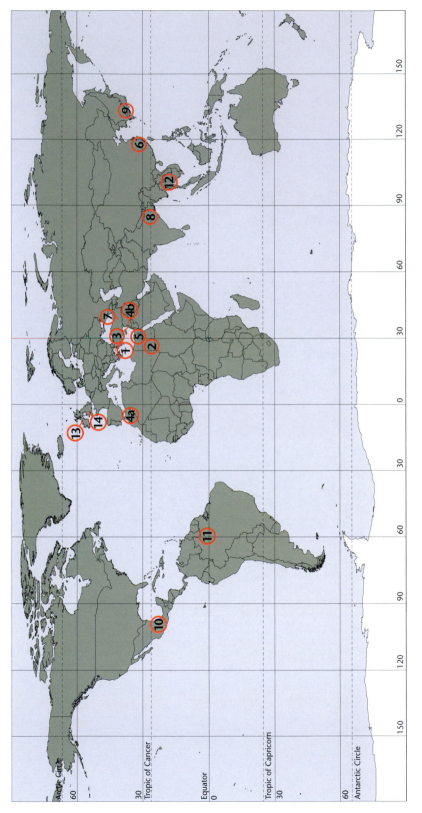

MAP 0 World map

TABLE 0.1 Geographic latitudes and longitudes of locations

1	Santorini, Greece	36.2	25.3
2	Dakhleh, Egypt	25.3	29.1
3	Beirut, Lebanon	33.5	35.3
4a	Fez, Morocco	34.3	-4.6
4b	Damascus, Syria	33.3	36.2
5	Cairo, Egypt	30.0	31.2
6	Zhouzhuang, China	30.5	120
7	Diyarbakır, Turkey	38.1	40.2
8	Baharampur, India	24.1	88.2
9	Kyoto, Japan	35.0	135.4
10	Mexico City, Mexico	19.2	-99.1
11	Manaus, Brazil	3.1	-60.0
12	Bangkok, Thailand	13.4	100.3
13	Belfast, Northern Ireland, UK	54.4	-6.0
14	Cardiff, Wales, UK	51.5	-3.2

Note: - is sign for West Longitude

Explanations for meteorological figures

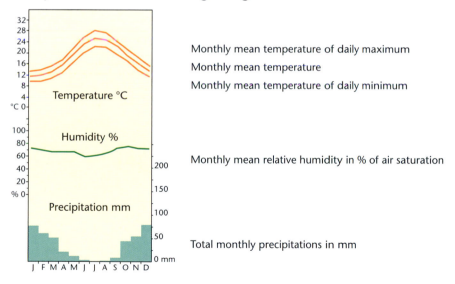

Monthly mean temperature of daily maximum

Monthly mean temperature

Monthly mean temperature of daily minimum

Monthly mean relative humidity in % of air saturation

Total monthly precipitations in mm

GRAPH 0 Explanations for meteorological figures

PART I

Bioclimatic Facets of Vernacular Architecture

1

THE FOUR ELEMENTS OF SANTORINI'S ARCHITECTURE

Thanos N. Stasinopoulos

Introduction

The four elements concept

According to a long line of scholars, from the ancient Greek philosophers to the medieval alchemists, the very essence of nature is a combination of four key elements in various configurations and interactions:

- ○ fire (e.g. sunlight, volcanoes);
- ⊕ earth (e.g. soil and most materials);
- ⊙ air (e.g. wind, oxygen);
- ⊖ water (e.g. sea, rain).

An obscure fifth element ('ether'?) of a rather spiritual nature is thought to bind the other four together, being the catalyst of life.

Greek philosophers linked these elements to the five Platonic solids, and Aristotle related the four main elements to our senses, with additional reference to the four seasons (Figure 1.1).

The philosophical aspects of the four elements are not the issue here; instead, it is their utilization as a systematic tool to look at architecture in relation to nature.

The vernacular settlements of Santorini are an excellent case to demonstrate that approach, as they offer numerous features at various scales that manifest the connection between the built environment and the four elements, exemplifying the influence of the natural forces

MAP 1 Santorini, Greece

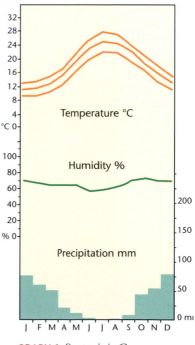

GRAPH 1 Santorini, Greece

| Fire | Earth | Air | Water | Ether |

FIGURE 1.1 The Platonic solids

in shaping architecture. From minute building details to entire neighbourhoods, from man-made structures to natural formations, Santorini seen through the 'four elements prism' highlights not only the power of nature but also the traditional response to natural conditions – and perhaps the effects of the contemporary lack of it.

The island of Santorini

Santorini or Thira is a striking natural example of the interaction between the four elements: it is a group of islands around the bay of Caldera, 90km north of Crete, remnants of a gigantic volcanic eruption (ca. 1500 BC) that obliterated the Minoan society of Crete with colossal tidal waves and a cataclysm of ash, perhaps also causing the natural phenomena described in Biblical *Exodus* (Figure 1.2).

FIGURE 1.2 The volcanic Caldera of Santorini; the dark islet in the middle was formed by eruptions as recent as 1950

Several scholars believe that Santorini was the legendary Atlantis that vanished due to a sudden natural disaster as described by Plato. Recent excavations have revealed a large settlement about thirty-five centuries old, well preserved under thick volcanic ash layers, which many believe is a trace of the famous lost civilization (Figure 1.3).

The landscape still bears clear marks of the great eruption: towards the crater there are steep red and black rock cliffs up to 300m high covered with light-coloured ash and pumice, and on the outer side there are smooth hills and long beaches with dark sand. The volcano remains active, as indicated by the sulphur-coloured warm water surfacing at the middle of Caldera bay, which is almost 400m deep.

Santorini climate

Climatic conditions are typical of the south Aegean region, with long sunshine and low precipitation. Humidity is fairly high even in summer due to the seawater mass, and for the same reason seasonal temperature fluctuations are rather limited generating mild winters and summers. Winds usually come from the north quite strongly – especially in winter – although the ones from the south can be fairly severe too. Despite the widespread perception of the Greek islands as warm places, the Santorini climate is rather cool during several months, and comfortable conditions can be improved by the intense solar radiation – but also worsened by the forceful winds (Figures 1.4 to 1.8).

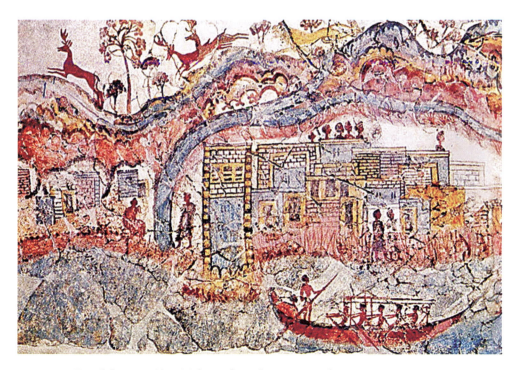

FIGURE 1.3 Detail from an Akrotiri fresco from the seventeenth century BC

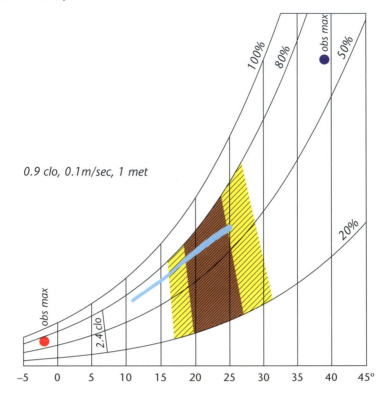

0.9 clo, 0.1m/sec, 1 met

FIGURE 1.4 Mean ambient temperature and humidity in Santorini lie within the comfort zone for most of the year, but with a substantial period on the cold side

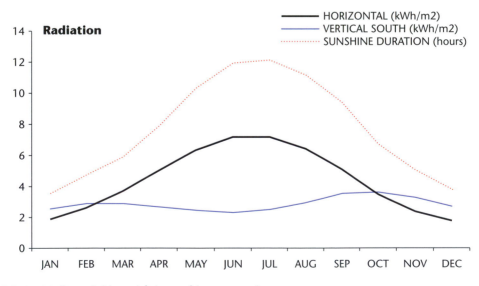

FIGURE 1.5 Santorini is as rich in sunshine as poor in water

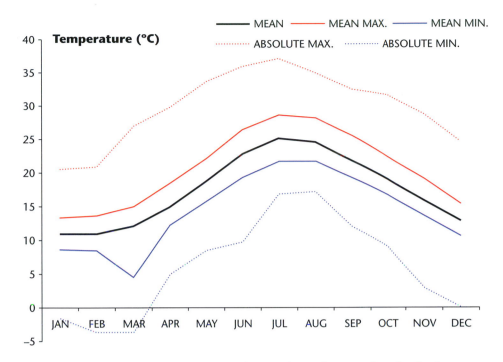

FIGURE 1.6 Mean ambient temperature exceeds 20°C during four months only; daytime temperatures can go much higher due to solar radiation

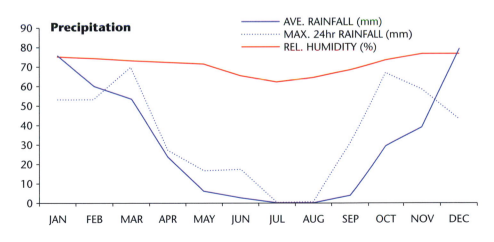

FIGURE 1.7 The sea mass sustains high relative humidity all year round; rainfall is rare during summer

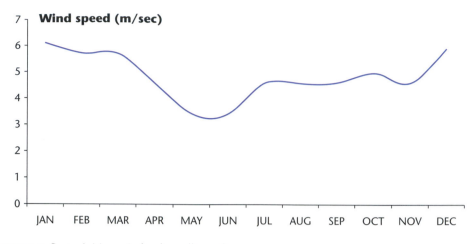

FIGURE 1.8 Santorini is a windy place all year long

Santorini architecture

The built fabric

The old settlements of Santorini – as in most small Aegean islands – are placed far from the shore: the fear of pirate assaults forced the locals to settle on steep cliffs or hidden valleys that offered better defence or were harder to spot from the sea (Figure 1.9). High density, narrow streets and small buildings have resulted from many factors: shortage of safe land, mutual protection from the wind and solar heat, security, family growth, saving of construction materials and the highly communal spirit of the old societies (Figure 1.10). In similar cases, for example, Mykonos and Astypalea, densities of up to one person per square metre have been reported, so we can imagine crammed conditions in Santorini too – without counting the numerous domestic animals, from chicken to donkeys.

Oia, a village of predominantly naval population at the north-west end of Santorini, features a layout clearly reflecting a hierarchical society: ship crews were living in crammed dwellings stacked on the steep cliff, while rich captains' mansions were occupying comfortable space on the flat top with far better daylight and ventilation conditions; both classes were at a 'safe' distance from the farmers of nearby village of Finikia (Figure 1.11).

Major building features

The buildings of Santorini resemble those in the rest of Cycladic islands: solid volumes, thick masonry walls with small openings, the whitewashed plaster skin covering almost everything with an integrative power, the creation of composition through continuous repetition (Figures 1.12 and 1.13).

All these elements have produced organic urban and building forms, evolving through a long response to the climatic conditions using the locally available resources and at the same time reflecting the social evolution through time (Figure 1.14).

FIGURE 1.9 Santorini houses resembling seagulls on the cliff top; a small anchorage below

FIGURE 1.10 An avalanche of whitewashed plaster

A particular ergonomic scale is evident, similar to the one found in ships: low doors, narrow and steep stairs, tiny inner/outer spaces. These are products of necessity rather than choice, since the dominant design rule was material and space minimalism (Figure 1.15).

Nature is the chief designer of that architectural idiom, imposing its whims on the local builders, i.e. the dwellers themselves in most cases. Climate, earthquakes, scarcity of materials and topography had been the primary design parameters, and were respected with admirable

FIGURE 1.11 Social hierarchy is reflected in spatial layout: captain mansions above crew dwellings

FIGURE 1.12 A typical vaulted house

integrity and ingenuity. Tradition resulting from long experience was dictating the building specifications from layout to decoration, with little ground for experiments or deviations from the established norms.

In such context, the introduction of neoclassical elements at the end of the nineteenth century must have been a radical act, adopted by rich captains who could afford showing off that they were following the new architectural style that was then flourishing in Europe (Figures 1.16 and 1.17).

FIGURE 1.13 A typical two-storey vaulted house; auxiliary rooms form a small yard protected from the wind; an open balcony offers view in calm weather

FIGURE 1.14 Organic forms: an outcome of necessities and time

FIGURE 1.15 Minimalist aerodynamic forms over the windswept sea

FIGURE 1.16 A typical façade of a captain's mansion; the wooden shutters are protected by large glazing

FIGURE 1.17
Elaborate mansion
windows

The four elements

Earth

Building materials

The main building material is the plentiful red or black lava stone, used with or without mortar and covered with plaster that protects the joints from the decay caused by wind and rain, also offering clearly visible evidence of cracks.

Although surrounded by the sea, Santorini is a very dry, windswept volcanic land hostile to vegetation, especially trees. As a result, timber had been a costly luxury, brought from distant places and over steep cliffs, which the locals used to construct items such as boats, furniture and doors rather than building elements such as roofs, lintels and wall ties.

The volcano has offered a compensation for the lack of structural timber: 'Theran soil', a volcanic ash with properties very similar to cement, had been widely used from ancient times to make mortar that was very strong, easily available and cheap (Figure 1.18).

Vaults

Given the scarcity of timber and the abundance of Theran soil, it is no wonder that the locals developed an architecture based on the compression strength of stone: the most common way to span large or small spaces was through quite thin vaulted roofs, bridging the gap between the much thicker sidewalls that withstand the horizontal forces of the vault (Figure 1.19).

This type of construction was so easy that it was applied in most buildings of every scale (Figures 1.20 and 1.21), even in very small ones (Figure 1.22). Today it has become the 'trademark' of Santorini, with many concrete replicas in spite of their higher cost than the original version.

FIGURE 1.18 Theran soil gives a powerful mortar that defies natural forces and time

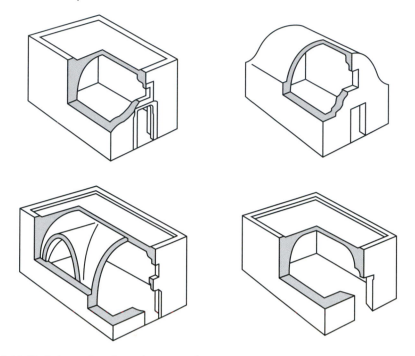

FIGURE 1.19 Variations of vaults and cross-vaults

Thin vaults offer little protection against solar heat coming from high altitude in summer or radiant losses to the clear night sky in winter, so they were often covered by a layer of pumice – another product of the volcano – enclosed in parapets that converted the curved top into a flat roof (Figure 1.23).

This made rainwater collection easier. Moreover, it was a way to show off wealth, since vaults were regarded as a too common and less 'classy' structure than timber flat roofs. For instance, the elaborate cross-vault ceilings of rich mansions are visible only from inside, as they have been hidden under 'flat' roofs (Figure 1.24).

As an extra sign of wealth, the upper half of the façades of these prominent buildings is often ornamented with exposed red masonry (Figure 1.25), which in less lavish houses is used only to outline openings. In less prestigious examples, the vaults are hidden behind free-standing rectangular parapets or even triangular gables, adding a 'neoclassical' flavour (Figure 1.26). The contemporary fashion (Figure 1.27) is ironic, given the past efforts to hide the vaults.

Volcano and earthquakes

A key feature of old masonry buildings in Santorini is their resistance to earthquakes: frequent tremors from the volcano are reminders of its presence, and traces of past calamities such as that of 1956 are still around. Aseismic rules shaped the overall geometry of the building, as well as of many details in plan and elevation, such as thick side walls and thin vaults, buttresses and tendons, narrow openings and rigid corners (Figure 1.28).

FIGURE 1.20 A dialogue of vaults

FIGURE 1.21 Vaults of various sizes and shapes

FIGURE 1.22 A tiny cross–vaulted storeroom in a field

FIGURE 1.23 A flat top over a vault with pumice infill in between

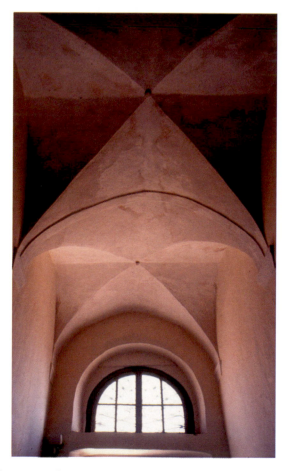

FIGURE 1.24 Multiple cross-vaults in a mansion; externally they are covered by a flat roof

FIGURE 1.25 Cross-section of an elaborate mansion that was half destroyed by an earthquake in 1956; the carved masonry façade and wooden railing were signs of wealth

FIGURE 1.26 Vaults hidden behind false façades

FIGURE 1.27 Contemporary flat roofs disguised as vaults

Excavated shelters

Santorini is one of the few places in Europe with troglodytes even today: the special properties of the ground, coupled with the necessity to economize on materials, led locals to excavate vaulted caves into the soft top layers of the volcanic ash. These are widely used as dwellings, stables (Figure 1.29), wineries or even churches (Figure 1.30). Their front was enclosed by masonry walls, frequently supporting the veranda of the next house up. The deep caves were typically divided into two or three rooms by partitions similar to the front elevations; the front room was for daytime use, with a bedroom and a storage room at the back (Figures 1.31 and 1.32). These are the best structures to withstand earthquakes, with the additional benefit of acting as free heating and cooling mechanisms due to the large thermal mass of earth.

FIGURE 1.28 Buttresses support a large vault covered by flat roof

FIGURE 1.29 Excavated stable with decorated entry

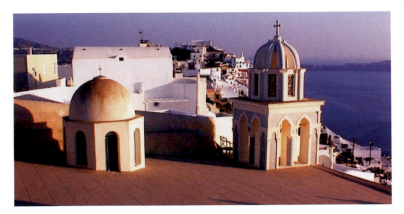

FIGURE 1.30 An excavated church; the flat top is used for rainwater collection

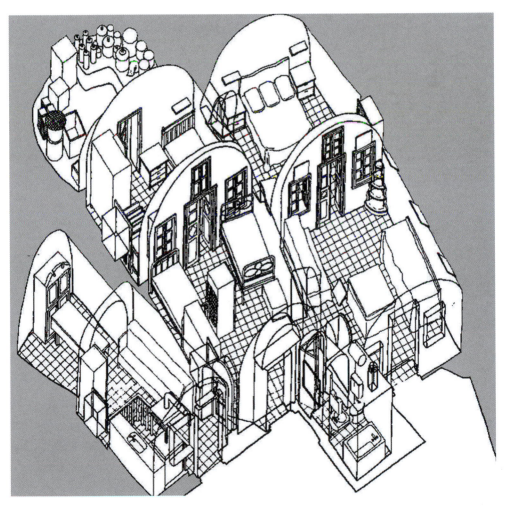

FIGURE 1.31 Excavated houses are often separated into two or three rooms with narrow façades on a common yard

FIGURE 1.32 Interior of an excavated house, looking in and out; internal partitions imitate the façade

Topography

Due to the steep ground, a vertical urban layout has been developed: the top of a house is frequently the veranda of the one above – or perhaps a public street (Figure 1.33). Thus an unusual three-dimensional property system has been adopted, requiring close cooperation between neighbours in issues such as construction, access and sewage (Figure 1.34). Needless to say, such a layout requires numerous stairs of many forms and sizes – and, of course, brave legs and hearts (Figure 1.35).

Recycling

The major construction difficulty, even today, has been the transport of materials over cliffs and steps with the only available – and best suited – means: donkeys and mules (Figure 1.36). It explains odd features such as massive rock chunks left on verandas or half-ruined walls merged into later structures, in order to bypass the hard task of taking the rubble away (Figure 1.37). The excavated walls of caves are sometimes 'adorned' by protruding rocks, left as they were found during construction in order not to alter the stability of the ground or to increase the transportation burden (Figure 1.38).

FIGURE 1.33 Excavated and built dwellings were stacked on the steep ground in a three-dimensional layout

FIGURE 1.34 Three-dimensional layout

FIGURE 1.35 A mélange of roofs, walls, terraces and stairs; most surfaces are used for rainwater collection

FIGURE 1.36 Traditional transport means – the only way to address the numerous steps

FIGURE 1.37 Old ruins embedded in a new elevation

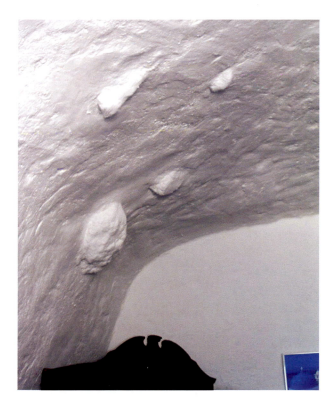

FIGURE 1.38 Rocks left on the excavated ceiling

Fire

Cooling

Solar radiation is quite intense in Santorini, especially in summer when clouds disappear for more than two months. Outdoor surfaces, whitewashed just before Easter, reduce the solar load on indoor spaces. At the same time, outdoor areas can become too uncomfortable due not only to solar heat coming from the sky, but also to heat reflected from the sunlit surfaces nearby, especially the light-coloured pavements. Discomfort is intensified by the blinding glare and the heat emitted from the warmed-up mass even after sunset; it is the summer northern winds that may bring relief, provided they are not too strong.

Pergolas and canopies require costly timber; they should also be rigid enough to withstand the forceful winds, thus becoming even more costly. Furthermore, water scarcity and the strong winds prohibit the growth of climbers. For those reasons, solar protection in outdoor spaces was offered only by the shade of adjacent buildings or free-standing walls – the same ones that were also used for wind protection. With such harsh conditions outdoors, it was only the dark indoor spaces which offered comfort in daytime, thanks to their heavy mass with low radiant temperature.

Heating

At the beginning of winter the reflectivity of the whitewashed surfaces is reduced by accumulated dust and the autumn rains. Solar heat would be welcome, but the small windows do not provide much indoors; occupant thermal comfort has to be achieved by other means.

Winter is rather chilly in Santorini, also humid and windy. The only fuel for space heating and cooking was in the form of bush branches, meticulously picked from the countryside. Small portable stoves were the only substitute for heavy clothes, metabolic heat or patience, since there were no fireplaces other than the ones in the kitchen.

However, due to the large heat capacity of the earth that dampens down diurnal and seasonal temperature fluctuations, a satisfactory level of thermal comfort can be achieved in the excavated dwellings during most of the winter, reducing the need for extra heating that is required mainly to lessen discomfort caused by humidity.

The small openings minimize heat losses, a vital benefit in the not so distant era when glass was a luxury for the few – if available at all; but at the same time they decrease natural light in the interior, where oil lamps and candles were left to provide the only light sources.

Water

Precipitation

Annual rainfall seldom exceeds 370mm in Santorini, and the volcanic earth hardly holds underground water reserves. Consequently plants survive mainly on air moisture in summer. As already said, the meagre vegetation offers limited firewood supplies and makes structural timber an exotic luxury.

Snow is another rarity, but humidity is a constant annoying factor, promoting mould growth in the dark, poorly ventilated caves. Additionally, it lessens indoor comfort, especially at the end of winter when the radiant temperature of the cave walls is at its lowest.

Domestic water and hygiene

Before the era of bottled water, water tankers and desalination, the precious liquid came only from the sky; hence rainwater collection was a decisive factor in the overall layout and form of each building – even churches or country houses (Figure 1.39). The typical dwelling had one or more underground cisterns where rainwater was collected from roofs and terraces via elaborate routes. Stored water was disinfected with a piece of limestone and was carefully withdrawn through a hatch over the cistern. Lime was also used to disinfect the water route, which had to remain free of animal droppings.

The washrooms were built away from the main quarters, usually above a small closet containing a collection tank; its contents – mixed with pumice – were periodically transported on donkeys to the fields outside the village as a man-made fertilizer (Figure 1.40).

A striking change today is the use of old cisterns as septic tanks, and also the addition of numerous swimming pools, again due to 'demand by visitors'.

FIGURE 1.39 A country chapel with cross vault and symmetrical facade; the rainwater cistern is located under the terrace

FIGURE 1.40 Typical toilets; sewage was collected in a basket

Air

Wind

Santorini is totally exposed to the frequent winds that sweep the Aegean Sea, a fact that local plants know all too well (Figures 1.41 and 1.42). It is only the cliffs around Caldera and small valleys that offer some protection, unless they face the incoming air stream where discomfort is intensified by the sand-blast effect caused by turbulence. Wind protection is of prime importance for outdoor living, as shown by many courtyards with raised walls or lowered floors where view has been sacrificed for sheltering (Figure 1.43).

Ventilation

Ventilation and daylight can be provided into the deep excavated caves only through their façade. The typical clerestory above the door lets the warm air escape, also letting in daylight

FIGURE 1.41 Trees pointing to the prevailing wind direction

FIGURE 1.42
Spiral vines withstand
strong winds

FIGURE 1.43 A small yard where the sea view has been sacrificed for wind protection

to the maximum depth possible. This is supplemented in some cases by vertical ducts through the ground above that admit air and light into the dark and unventilated rooms.

Lack of heating and limited ventilation trigger condensation; this happens even more so in the excavated vaults that are surrounded by the moisture of the soil. It is easy to imagine the unhealthy living conditions under such circumstances; considering also the chronic water shortages and the co-existence with numerous animals, one should have a smelly rather than an idyllic picture of everyday life in the past.

Conclusion

If Santorini is to be appreciated, it is not because of its 'poetic' forms or breathtaking vistas: aside from aesthetics, living conditions in the past were not very attractive for the other senses or for one's health. The architecture that we cherish today as 'picturesque' is in fact the product of a long struggle for survival in an adverse environment by generations who have managed to squeeze their means out of the available natural resources in a sustainable manner. What should really be honoured is the fact that the locals adapted their notion of comfort and other needs to the local setting, and merged the effects of the four elements into an honest, minimalist architectural idiom, thus offering a brilliant example of vernacular environmental sustainability (Table 1.1). Perhaps here we should contemplate the fifth element as the spirit and ingenuity of the locals who have created and sustained life out of the other four.

Remarks

- Climatic data in this paper is from Greek National Meteorological Service (EMY); measurements 1931–40, 1954–56, 1960–70.
- Thanos has added his own data to the psychometric chart, the comfort zone in Figure 1.4 is after (or based on) Markus, T. A. and Morris, E. N. (1980) *Buildings, climate and energy*, London, Pitman.

TABLE 1.1 Relation between the four elements and features of Santorini architecture

	Fire	*Water*	*Air*	*Earth*
layout	dense fabric for mutual shading		dense fabric for mutual wind protection	stepped back due to topography
building types				excavated masonry vaults
layout features	yards for shade	terraces for rainwater collection	yards for wind protection	narrow and deep spaces
materials	Theran soil for mortar pumice for insulation	no water? no timber!	robustness needed, to withstand wind	soil easy to dig large variety of stones difficult transport
walls	heat capacity dampens temperature swings		wind protection plastered to avoid decay	earthquake horizontal vault forces
roofs	insulated with pumice	no timber? vaults! rainwater collection	heavy to avoid uplift	covered with pumice
windows	small size reduces heat transfer	arched lintels	shutters behind glazing for wind protection	small size to avoid wall weakening
forms	compact to minimize fabric heat flow	curved structures with compression materials only rainwater channelling affects geometry	aerodynamic shapes and details reduce wind effects	compact to save materials aseismic rules dictate geometry embedded rubble and rocks to reduce transport
heating	minimal direct gain	no fuel for heating, just for cooking moisture lessens indoor comfort	wind may reduce comfort	thermal mass augments indoor air temperature in early winter
cooling	high reflectivity reduces solar load warm mass emits heat	no timber for shading no climbers for shading moisture enhances indoor comfort	wind may improve comfort strong winds damage shading devices	thermal mass absorbs heat, improving indoor comfort
ventilation	clerestories expel warm air	dampness and mould due to limited ventilation	clerestories and air ducts enhance air movement	limited in caves
daylight	small openings sufficient for summer daylight clerestories admit daylight more deeply			limited in caves
watering		rainwater collection plants surviving on moisture		no water reserves in volcanic ground

2

A LESSON IN URBAN DESIGN FROM DAKHLEH OASIS

Riccardo Balbo

MAP 2 Dakhleh, Egypt

Introduction

The environmental approach

Throughout time, and in all cultures, architecture has been directly linked to resource availability. Resources have been a fundamental influence on the forms of built structures and this still serves as a valid paradigm. An appropriate definition of Islamic architecture may be as an ante litteram synthetic expression of functionalism and sustainable design. This is a possible definition that results from considering how Islamic architecture is the outcome of logical, functional design, customized and adapted to the environment and to local resources and materials, responsive to harsh climatic conditions while adhering with the well-defined principles of Islam. The Islamic definition of environment embraces the territory; nature and humans shape and organize the territory and thereby produce the environment. Egyptian Islamic architecture is a product determined by the harsh and dry climate, by Islamic culture, by the Bedouin and Berbers' peaceful trading and aggressive incursions, by the slave trade from Sudan to the Americas, with all of this occurring in a wide, deserted, hilly territory with scarce water and building resources. Another important factor is the study and application of the principles of the *Holy Q'ran,* which have undeniably shaped Islamic architecture. As this practice affects the concept of overall Muslim life, it is possible to investigate how behavioural religious

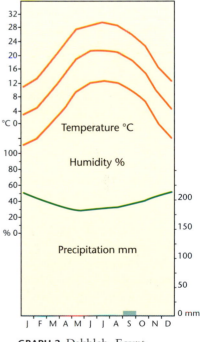

GRAPH 2 Dakhleh, Egypt

principles have shaped towns, villages and houses. The work presented here is based on an ongoing research project on the study of mud brick settlements built in the twelfth and thirteenth centuries in the Dakhleh Oasis, Egypt.

The location

The oasis

The Dakhleh Oasis (25° 30'N and 29° 07'E) is one of the five principal oases in the western desert of Egypt. Situated approximately 800km SSE of Cairo, surrounded by the empty expanse of the Eastern Sahara, it measures some 80km from east to west and has a maximum width of 25km. Due to the extreme arid conditions of the Sahara Desert, the source of water at the western desert oasis is from artesian wells and underground pressure. In 1819, Sir Archibald Edmonstone was the first European traveller to 'discover' the Dakhleh Oasis. However, it was not until 1908 – when Herbert Winlock, one of the first Egyptologists, visited the oasis – that the characteristics of the monuments, the architecture and the structure of villages and cities were systematically noted, and apart from travellers' reports of the nineteenth and early twentieth centuries, little has been written on the history and architecture of the Dakhleh Oasis.

Case studies

The first task of the on-site research was to explore the villages in the oasis.[1] Two villages, Al Qasr and Balat, were chosen as case studies owing to the richness of their architectural and urban features. Al Qasr is a fortified village, built on top of an arid hill with an excellent view over the desert and good visibility of far off sand tracks. The southern slope extends smoothly to the flat sand zone, where ancient artesian wells provide the water. The northern side of the hill opens to the plateau leading to the Farafra Oasis. The original settlement of earthen architecture was preserved intact and this allowed the village to grow vertically during its most prosperous period. The process was similar to that observed in southern and central European towns in the Middle Ages, where cities that were constrained by natural boundaries or defensive walls could only expand vertically by adding to the existing settlement or demolishing entire districts and rebuilding them at higher density. Most Italian cities and villages can be observed to show indications of such expansion, which demonstrates how strong the defensive attitude of the community was and how this limited the idea of the city beyond its original boundaries. Just as in Europe the Napoleonic war campaigns had made defensive structures useless in Italy, similarly in these desert regions as soon as the massive Bedouin raids stopped after the Second World War the mostly abandoned settlement gave way to an alternative development with a new generation of houses built outside the remains of the fortified walls.

By comparison, Balat, positioned on a less marked ridge and closer to a water source, was more expansive, probably due to its lower economic rank. The architecture and urban morphology, even if derived from the same principles and systems, show a rural origin and in some respects are indicators of an earlier stage of development than Al Qasr. However, it too was abandoned in the late 1980s.

Factors of strength and weakness

The most important concern for the settlements was their distance from sources of water. In this region *ezbas* are small mud brick buildings and rural houses located close to the agricultural fields and in the surroundings of the main villages, where farmers organize the work in the fields and where wells and stables are situated. Their location was closely related to the availability of water. In Al Qasr, which is built on the top of a hill with good defensive systems, the need for water forced the population to travel to *ezbas* daily (especially in the driest seasons) in order to collect water for household use (Figure 2.1). In Balat the distance from water was not such a prominent issue.

The geomorphology of the area was responsible for the better conservation of the Al Qasr settlement. It prevented the water table from rising, which could have caused the destruction of the earthen structural foundations. An example of such an event occurred several years ago when a short winter rain completely destroyed numerous buildings. The Al Qasr community that chose to establish the village far from water for strategic and status reasons demonstrated its ability to control waste, as well as showing respect for the existing structures built over time. The houses that were built, rebuilt, transformed, enlarged, divided and conceived to satisfy the inhabitants' needs are important lessons in architectural and urban sustainable design.

The urban structure

The urban morphology

In all likelihood the two fundamental issues of importance in the evolution of Islamic architecture were the concepts of privacy and the view of women's role in the family and in society. This led Islamic urban morphology to have a three-layered organization: private,

FIGURE 2.1 Al Qasr *ezba*

private-public and public. The original shape of the urban nucleus during the Islamic Period had different characteristics from what we currently refer to as the Arab fortified village. Initially, houses were single storey in order to respect and reflect the religious notion of equality between people in society. This influence is still visible today in the village of Balat. It can be traced back to the sacred book of Islam. The consistent height of the houses can be linked to the refusal to waste one's abundance. It is immoral to show off one's richness and it is avoided as a sign of respect for the neighbourhood and the community that might be offended:

> O children of Adam, wear your beautiful apparel at every time and place of prayer, eat and drink, but waste not by excess, for God loveth not the wasters.
>
> Surat Al-'A 'rāf (7,31)

The *Holy Q'ran* constantly reminds Muslims that while man is allowed to enjoy the pleasures of the private dimension of life in calm, excesses, showing off and the frivolous waste of resources are contrary to the will of Allah:

> They will question thee concerning what they should expend. Say: 'the abundance'.
>
> Surat Al-Baqarah (2,219)

Yet, as always, the deep integration between ethnicity, culture and available resources is evident. Differences in house elevation might deprive neighbours of refreshing breezes and the benefit drawn from the shape of adjoining or facing houses:

> Do you know the rights of a neighbour; you must not build to exclude the breeze from him unless you have his permission.
>
> (Hakim, 1979)

With the same attention and sensitivity, the width of connecting public streets was regulated in order to integrate different aspects:

> If you disagree about the width of a street, make it seven cubits.
>
> (Ibid. 1 cubit = 50cm)

Two-storey buildings could receive light on both sides without mutual deprivation. In addition, the width of a minor street was considered inadequate for trade and commerce, which usually employed donkeys, horses and camels for transport. However, the most important issue was to avoid situations that could compromise a family's privacy due to insufficient distance from adjacent buildings (Figure 2.2).

On the other hand, the privacy distance should not be exceeded because wider streets could be detrimental to the defence of the village and weaken the urban control exercised by locals. This principle was still applicable where a narrower street might have benefits in terms of improved airflow. Other secondary streets, such as cul-de-sacs and semi-private alleys, served family groups or women who were segregated from the men and had to use different access routes. Neighbourhoods also had to provide access for the delivery of goods:

> If a man is walking in the street and finds a branch of thorns and removes it, then God will thank him and forgive him.
>
> Riyadh as-Salihin (13,127)

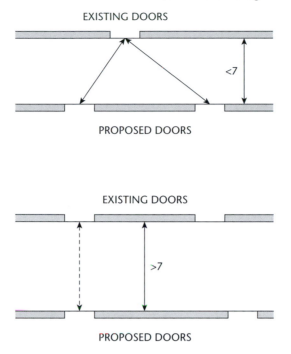

FIGURE 2.2 Relationship between street width and privacy

As any kind of socialization between men and women outside the family was forbidden, the interiors of houses had separate spaces and paths reserved respectively for females and males. The *madiafa* was a room dedicated to male meetings. Internal gateways were added to the external ones to control access and to protect the quarters from enemies, predators and strong winds. All of these privacy features are also connected to bioclimatic factors relating to urban morphology and housing typology. The placement of openings was determined by their dimensions, their position on the façade and whether they were facing other openings (Figures 2.3 and 2.4). The purpose of openings was to let light and air enter while preventing strangers and merchants from seeing the women in the house:

> He who looks into a house without the occupants' permission, and they puncture his eyes, will have no rights to demand a fine or ask for punishment.
>
> (Hakim, 1979)

On the other hand, openings at different levels on opposite façades of buildings guaranteed a refreshing indoor effect thanks to natural air convection. By alternating the position of openings on the façade (for the Islamic house, there is no proper 'main' façade) natural ventilation was assured on both daily and seasonal cycles. The *masharabyia* (Figure 2.5) was associated with the upper openings, which stopped the wandering eyes of outsiders from penetrating while still allowing women to look outside without being seen. It has a peculiar shape, and the concept involves a system that accelerates the air stream and drives it towards a clay jar, or *olla* (Figure 2.6), that is filled with water that transpires through the pores of the *olla*, humidifying and cooling the air and thus improving indoor thermal comfort.

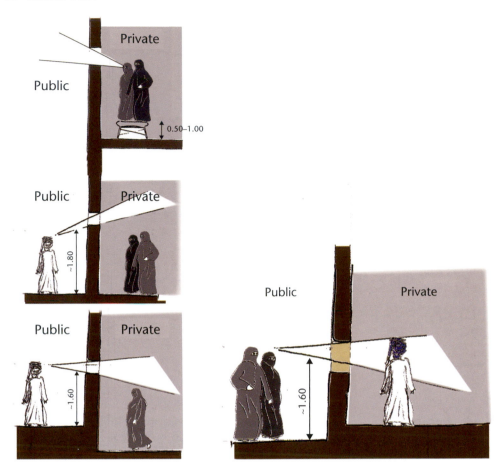

FIGURE 2.3 Vertical window positioning and privacy

FIGURE 2.4 Shop window positioning

Vertical growth

The need for space

During the long Islamic and *Fatimith* period, the *Holy Q'ran* stipulated that towns and buildings were to be built to one fixed height, usually of one or two storeys, and had to avoid any ornamentation or decoration in order to pay respect to the dignity and freedom of other Muslims. They had to observe rights to light and air and had to allow the *Mohazzin*'s voice to travel unhindered to reach everyone's home. As time passed, demographic increases and economic development forced the community to expand into new vertical models, yet still without consideration of plots outside the boundary walls for new additions to the settlement:

> Of happiness: a good wife, a spacious home, a good neighbour and a good mount.
> Al-Hakim, Abu-Nu 'aym and Al-Bayhaqi (7,94)

FIGURE 2.5 *Masharabyia*   **FIGURE 2.6** *Olla*

The collective demand for space gradually led to the addition of floors to existing buildings. Both the community and individual citizens engaged in a continual negotiation that radically transformed the urban morphology. This even led to the sale and building-up of space above public streets, as a result making them appear narrower due to the increase in building height.

The labyrinth-like town

As the raised and cantilevered buildings became more common, the townscape changed into an endless and dangerous labyrinth (Figure 2.7). The raised building, or *sabat* (literally 'the rest'), weakened the urban fabric of 'house-façade-street'. At the same time it introduced innovative essential characteristics that evolved in response to the harsh desert climate. A first interesting feature was the niche and small opening above the door of every room. The niche was for candles, and the opening allowed air circulation even when doors were closed. The new design allowed many houses to open simultaneously both onto the street and onto two inner courts with exposure on opposite sides. This provided the best conditions for natural ventilation. There was evidence also of the Coranic principle of sharing resources with neighbours. A common application was the sharing of walls to support the wooden cantilevered palm tree beams over the street:

> A neighbour should not forbid his neighbour to insert wooden beams in his wall.
>
> (Hakim, 1979)

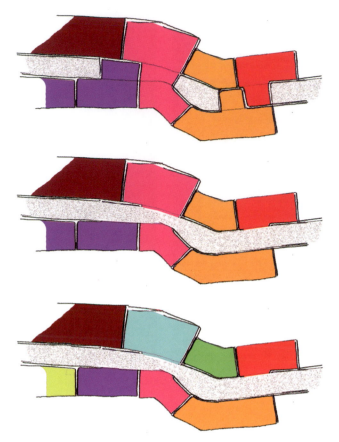

FIGURE 2.7 Town labyrinth structure growing process

The hot climate called for doubled thickness of the main mud brick walls for thermal resistance as well as to support the increased weight (Figure 2.8). The religious principles and trading common sense forbade one to stop or hesitate along the streets. Gatherings and chatting in public spaces threatened privacy and might also hinder or obstruct the circulation of goods:

> 'Avoid sitting on thoroughfares' (they said it is difficult to avoid doing so as it is our gathering place where we spend time talking) 'but if you insist, then you should respect the rights of thoroughfares' (what are these rights they asked) 'avoid staring, do not create harm, salute back those who salute you, bid to honour and forbid dishonour'.
>
> (Hakim, 1979)

The setting up of temporary shelters or tents for merchants may redirect or prevent the cool breeze. This explains the existence of the *madiafa*, a space dedicated to gatherings of small groups of adult males. This semi-public room is within the house boundary where the family opens itself to the neighbourhood, to guests and to merchants, hosting them in the night while women disappear into the secret innermost part of the home. The *madiafa* remains

FIGURE 2.8 Double walls for cantilevered structures

the most representative place for the family group, placed aside of the main entrance even up to the present day, as one still finds in most Islamic private residences:

> O ye who believe, enter not houses, other than your own, until ye have asked permission and saluted those in them: that is best for you, in order that ye may heed.
>
> Surat An-Nūr (24,27)

The only alternative for gatherings was the *Jamaa'* (the Mosque) and the *madrasa*, an educational institution where all subjects were taught according to Islamic principles. The Al Qasr *madrasa* dates back to the tenth century, before the existence of mosques, and has a main congregation hall of double height that served as both lecture room and prayer hall.

Moving outside

With the *sabat* the town provided plenty of covered outdoor public places, shaded from the sun and refreshed by the breeze that accelerated through the narrower points of the built-up alleys (Figure 2.9). In conjunction with the *sabat* the Islamic town also introduced another important urban element: the *m'qad*, the public resting place. Benches with double-height steps built of the same mud bricks and plastered in gentle, smooth forms were placed under the *sabat* to allow people to gather and enjoy the breeze. The *sabat* refers etymologically to 'sabbatical', resting by a cool, shaded place. Increasing lack of space led to use of the roof top for sleeping, to store wheat and dry food or even to breed chickens. In many cases a proper oven was added for baking bread. A toilet, or *hammam*, (always oriented perpendicular to the Holy direction) is also found there. To maintain privacy, long palm tree branches were used as natural fences. When more privacy was required, mud brick walls were built, with holes to let the people look out and to let the breeze through.

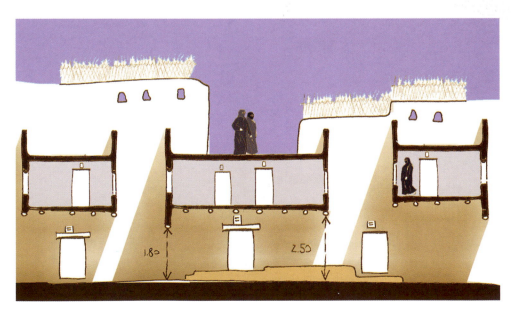

FIGURE 2.9 Shaded alleys, light wells, *sabat*

Light wells

In the wealthier towns such as Al Qasr, the vertical expansion was so considerable that it covered long parts or even entire internal streets, building up to three storeys above ground level, and in some cases creating very dark passages (Figure 2.10). The only possible solution, to reduce this tunnel effect, was to break the continuity of the *sabat* to let natural light penetrate (Figures 2.11 and 2.12). All of the surrounding openings were allowed to open onto these light wells, as light and wind still remained a right for every Muslim. Allowing the sun back into the dark alleys also helped the natural circulation of air.

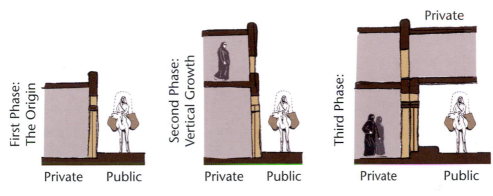

FIGURE 2.10 Three phases in the town's growth

FIGURE 2.11 A sequence of light wells

FIGURE 2.12 *Sabat* with *m'qad*, Balat

Conclusions

Al Qasr provides urban designers and architects with considerations of the value of local culture and environment, and how relations between them are intertwined. The delicate equilibrium between socio-economic and political aspects of an urban environment with microclimatic characteristics can easily be disrupted when one aspect becomes more prominent than others. Therefore, any kind of human intervention – and all its possible ramifications – should be carefully considered. A responsible, sustainable architecture should be ethical, should use the scarce resources as a starting point and should succeed in its goal of 'do not waste'. In architecture a question is: building knowledge or living knowledge? This study demonstrates that urban design and architectural projects should be considered as insertions of sentences in an already written book, with rules, meanings and quotations. To paraphrase the philosopher M. Heidegger, only if we are able to inhabit, can we build and dwell properly – 'building, dwelling, thinking'.

Acknowledgements

This work presents the partial results of research carried out in Egypt during the summer of 2005 by the author along with the architect Francesca De Filippi and with the assistance of P. Viotti, F. Picciau, N. Abdel Karim and M. T. De Paola. This study is also documented in a PhD thesis edited by Francesca De Filippi. Photographs and drawings are by the author.

Notes

1 'Learning from Tradition: Improving and Implementing Sustainable Building Methods and Techniques oriented to Conservation of Indigenous Architecture in the New Valley Region', collaborative project between the Politecnico di Torino (Italy) and Assyut University (Egypt) funded by the Italian and Egyptian Ministries of Foreign Affairs.

Reference

Hakim, B. S. (1979) *Arabic – Islamic Cities*, London, Kegan Paul.

3

WINDOWS AS ENVIRONMENTAL MODIFIERS IN THE VERNACULAR ARCHITECTURE OF LEBANON

Habib Melki

MAP 3 Beirut, Lebanon

Introduction

Lebanese architecture was greatly influenced by the abundance of stone, which offered the opportunity for good masonry construction. This produced families of stonemasons who passed on their accumulated skill from generation to generation, evolving a mastery and tradition of design in stone that is largely responsible for the homogeneous character of Lebanese architecture (Figure 3.1). Windows, a major detail of this construction, were meticulously placed according to sun orientation, topography, wind patterns, views and socio-cultural aspects (Figure 3.2). Windows are the least effective heat flow inhibitors of a building's shell, both in terms of letting heat out in the winter and letting heat in during the summer.

The evolution of the window in traditional Lebanese architecture shows an evident change in size, form and function. The factors that affected this evolution were not only technological but also cultural, arising from the standing of different social classes in Lebanese society. The progression of window typologies was clearly reflected in the larger cities, Beirut, Tripoli and Sidon. The treatment of the wall in terms of surface area, thickness and materiality remained a primary concern that evolved with changes in window design. Window openings were minimized to be consistent with interior requirements and were recessed (Figure 3.3a and Figure 3.3b). Different openings were provided for cross-ventilation or to get the benefit of prevailing summer winds and were sized accordingly (Figure 3.4).

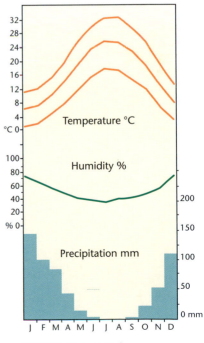

GRAPH 3 Beirut, Lebanon

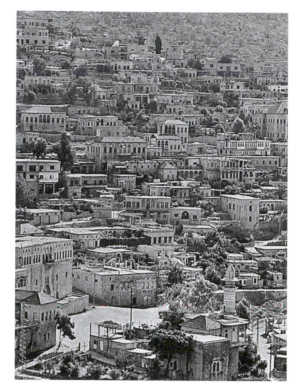

FIGURE 3.1 Lebanese village, Hasbaya

Source: Ragette, 1980, p.164

FIGURE 3.2 Site and topography, Qoahayya–Assia–Balaa

FIGURE 3.3a Small windows, North Lebanon   **FIGURE 3.3b** Recessed window, Amsheet

FIGURE 3.4 Rectangular house, South Lebanon

Climatic aspects

Climate in Lebanon is characterized by a cold winter season (January–March), a hot summer season (July–September) and two mild mid-seasons (April–June and October–December). The climatic regions are defined as follows:

Zone 1   Coastal 0–700m;
Zone 2   Western Mid-Mountain 700–1400m;
Zone 3   Inland Plateau 700–1150m;
Zone 4   High Mountain Littoral side + 1400m – Inland side + 1150m.
Climate Zoning for Buildings in Lebanon (UNDP, 2005)

The diverse topographic characteristics of these regions result in different site-specific situations (Figure 3.5). The configuration of hills and valleys affects relative humidity as well as the orientation of sites with respect to sun and wind. Wind direction is from the coast into the valley during daytime, reversing at night. Consequently, all sites flanking the valley have wind flow patterns that depend on location, altitude and time of day.

Social, cultural and economic factors

Throughout history, Lebanon was the crossroads of a variety of cultures and civilizations. These currents, coming from both East and West, carried new forms; concepts merged with local tradition to evolve what we currently know as Lebanese architecture. New technologies

FIGURE 3.5 Site and topography, Bsharry, North Lebanon

and socio-cultural aspects copied from the West mixed with the Arab identity to contribute to the development of the Lebanese identity in architectural forms (Liger–Belair, 2000, p.169). The evolution of Lebanese society and its definitive classes was directly translated into the architectural language. The poor continued living in the simple cubic structures, with minimal decorative window features (Figure 3.6), while the rich, depending on their social and financial standings occupied the 'Beirutie' House (middle class) or the mansion (high class) (Figure 3.7).

FIGURE 3.6 Simple rectangular house and window, Ham

FIGURE 3.7 Quartier Sursok – Beirut

The arch-shaped windows and the introduction of columns in the configuration are indications of Roman, Italian and Venetian influences from different periods. Whether through conquerors, artists or architects invited by the Emirs, new trends, forms and decorative patterns were introduced and added to define the typical Lebanese style (Figure 3.8). With the spread of Islam the concept of protecting the woman from outsiders introduced the *moucharabieh* and reduced the size and number of windows. The Roman arched window borrowed new features from the Islamic style and became the pointed arched window, a particularity of Lebanese architecture (Sehnaaoui, 2002, p.85) (Figure 3.9).

During the second part of the nineteenth century, major cities in Lebanon – Beirut especially – became trade centres; the influence of foreigners who settled there on a permanent basis revolutionized the concept of the window. Its small protective character gave way to the big exposed window, not only to see out but also to be seen. The new façades with large openings giving views towards the sea or the street were definitely an evident rupture with the past. The triple arched façades were an indication of the appearance of a new social class: the trade bourgeoisie (Figure 3.10). Although different religious groups had their own preferences in architectural styles, ornamentation was mainly used for its originality and innovation (Figure 3.11). The use of glass in Lebanon was mentioned for the first time in 1847 by H. Guys, who clearly indicated that it was found solely in rich houses. Boyer describes these façades as being oriented in the direction of the main street or to a garden or court,

FIGURE 3.8 Lebanese window, Qozhayya, Wadi Qannoubine

FIGURE 3.9a Pointed arch style (exterior), Jezzine

FIGURE 3.9b Pointed arch style (interior), Beirut

FIGURE 3.10a Central Bay – continuity and change

FIGURE 3.10b Palace Joumblat, Moukhtara

Source: Saliba, 1998, p.55

FIGURE 3.11a Variations in triple arch windows, Ehden

FIGURE 3.11b Variations in triple arch windows, Beit El-Dine

FIGURE 3.12 Stained glass windows, Beit El-Dine

supported by white marble columns with meticulous details in the woodwork and the occasional use of coloured glass, which made the window a real piece of art (Sehnaaoui, 2002, p.85). (Figure 3.12).

The design quality in the composition, the detailing and the amount of ornamentation reflected the wealth and social standing of households. However, with the spread of rental houses and increased demand for construction of moderate cost the master builders were able to apply the ornament vocabulary more widely. Mass produced ornamentation and spontaneous collage of different elements slowly replaced the elaborate, refined and unique designs (Saliba, 1998, p.42) (Figure 3.13).

Window typologies

From the middle of the twentieth century, Lebanon witnessed a gradual disappearance and dissolution of vernacular structures. A closer study of these dwellings may highlight the variation of different window typologies and their details, encompassing perfect adaptation to climate and site and intelligent use of local resources (Figure 3.14).

Rectangular windows

The rectangular window is the simplest and most common form (Figure 3.15a and Figure 3.15b). Applied in all house typologies, the rectangular window evolved from a small, thick and roughly constructed opening to an elaboration of ornaments and fine details (refer to Figure 3.10). The oldest window–shaped opening recorded in Lebanese history goes back to prehistoric times, where natural caves were enclosed to create living spaces (Figure 3.16).

FIGURE 3.13 Fakhry Building – continuity and change

Source: Saliba, 1998, p.60

FIGURE 3.14 Site adaptation, Wadi Qannoubine

FIGURE 3.15a Simple rectangular window (exterior), Baalbek

FIGURE 3.15b Simple rectangular window (interior), Baalbek

FIGURE 3.15c Simple rectangular window, Ehden

Section AA′

Section BB′

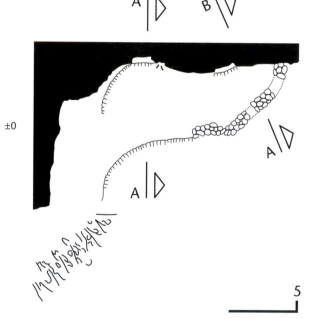

FIGURE 3.16 Drawings: two sections and floor plan

Source: Corpus Levant, 2004

A masonry wall of dry stacked stones, some 80cm thick, was erected along the opening of the cave up to a certain height controlled by needs of defence, natural light and ventilation (Figure 3.17). Additional openings were dug into the mountain for cross ventilation. Orientation was dictated by the natural setting of the caves. This typology evolved into a primitive form of seasonal housing (Figure 3.18), mainly for cattle and sheep breeding, characterized by its cylindrical shape with one rectangular window of 80 by 80cm and the main entry (low door) positioned to avoid dominant winds (Figure 3.19).

A more elaborate and permanent form of vernacular architecture, found in all regions, was the rectangular house. This is the simplest type of flat-roofed dwelling dating from 5000 years BC (Figure 3.20). The windows of the rectangular house were defined by the masonry walls, 50–100cm thick, which included niches and storage areas, and were limited in number and size according to climatic region. Lintels were of monolithic stone blocks or wooden elements (Figure 3.21). No protrusions were evident, and smaller openings located above these windows (below the roof) served as ventilators (closed during winter). Deciduous trees and scaffoldings supporting deciduous vines helped block sunlight in summer. Overhangs were later introduced as shading devices and to keep rainwater away from walls and windows. The thick, sometimes tapered, walls were carefully designed to shade the opening in summer but not block sunlight in winter (Figure 3.22). The use of wooden external shutters was also a means of shading (Figure 3.23). The orientation of these windows followed the natural setting since site integration and minimum excavation ruled the positioning and shape of the house.

On the coastal region, where solar gain and humidity are factors for consideration, windows were placed for maximum ventilation. By contrast, in the high-mountain region, the number and size of windows were kept to a minimum (Figure 3.24). Open spaces on

FIGURE 3.17 Troglodyte dwelling at Ras Chekka

Source: Corpus Levant, 2004

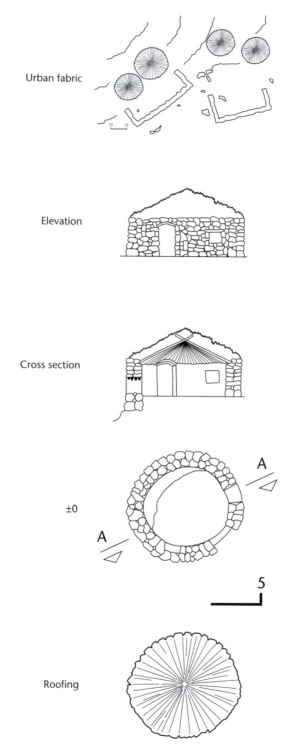

Urban fabric

Elevation

Cross section

±0

5

Roofing

FIGURE 3.18 Drawings: site plan, elevation, section, floor plan and roof plan

Source: Corpus Levant, 2004

FIGURE 3.19 Shepherd's shelter

Source: Corpus Levant, 2004

West Elevation

Floor Plan

Section A-A

FIGURE 3.20
House with an
interior arcade

Source: Ragette p.19

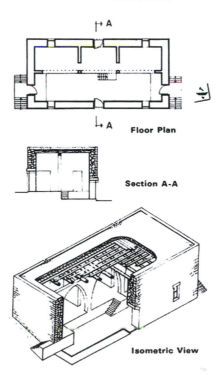

Isometric View

FIGURE 3.21 Rectangular house exterior and interior

FIGURE 3.22 Tapered walls, Deir Al-Amar

the north side of buildings were usually reserved for summertime outdoor activities in all climatic regions of the country. In inland areas, window openings were few because of the characteristic grouping of houses minimizing exposure. In the Beqa'a, close groupings of rectangular houses predominate and detached houses are rare (Ragette, 1980, p.22). In the high-mountain region, building into the sloped hillside or providing a berm (the level area separating ditch from bank on a hill-fort or barrow) were means for reducing exposure to the elements (Figures 3.25a and 3.25b). The development of this typology of Lebanese houses focused on two major architectural features: view and protection from undesirable climatic conditions. With summer outdoor activities centred on the open spaces to the north of the house, this became the dominant orientation of the gallery (the *riwaq,* an arcade or portico open on at least one side) (Figure 3.26) with views towards a valley to gain the pleasant breeze

FIGURE 3.23 Wooden shutters, Deir Al–Amar

FIGURE 3.24 Ebel Es Saqi, South Lebanon

FIGURE 3.25a Hermel

FIGURE 3.25b Chebaa

for natural cooling. The gallery was designed to act as sun screen in summer and as sunny area for the cold seasons, while keeping the area protected from the rain (Figures 3.27).

On both single-storey and two-storey houses the larger window openings are found in stone walls of lesser thickness (40–50cm) (Figure 3.28). Smaller openings were placed above or adjacent to larger windows and served for ventilation and daylighting in the cooler seasons, and for when the house was left unoccupied (Figure 3.29). Lighting accessories such as lamps and candles used to light the area of the *riwaq* at night have special small niches on the side walls. The *riwaq* was used for social activities during the mild and summer seasons. It also

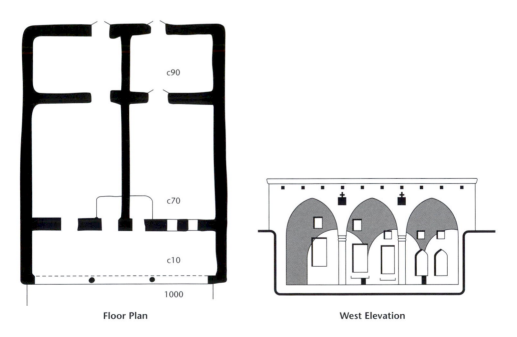

Floor Plan

West Elevation

FIGURE 3.26 House 1, Younine

Source: Ragette, 1980, p.39

FIGURE 3.27 Jezzine House

FIGURE 3.28 The gallery house, *riwaq*

Source: Ragette, 1980, p.38

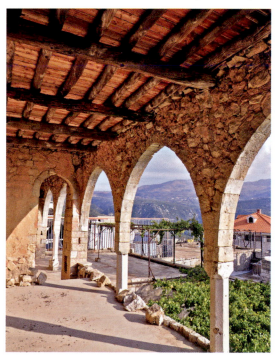

FIGURE 3.29 Gallery house, Hasbaya

served as a connecting passage of the house. It is greater in length than in depth and serves several rooms while being connected to the entrance of the house. Its height is the same as that of the rooms at about 4.0–5.0 metres (Ragette, 1980, p.39) (Figure 3.30).

The *liwan* is a covered porch surrounded by living spaces but open to the outside (Ragette, 1980, p.68). Seldom found in the high mountain region, the *liwan* is used for circulation, social activities and for storage (Figure 3.31). Cross-ventilation was achieved by internal windows or vents opening to the *liwan* (Figure 3.32). The position of this central space ensured that this was the coolest space of the house during daytime in summer. Shielded on its long sides by the adjacent rooms, the open end of the hall was oriented either to the north or to the south. Light coloured materials were used on exterior surfaces to reflect solar radiation in summertime and maximize the use of natural lighting. Other criteria that played a role in selecting the position of the openings were views, natural lighting and privacy requirements. The construction was usually of bearing walls composed of two ashlar stone faces and a rubble core totalling some 60–100cm in thickness. The width of the openings is spanned by stone lintels or arches. The liwan is vaulted like the rest of the house (Ragette, 1980, p.84).

As a rule, orientation of openings is towards the view down the valley; the side of the house carries several windows and offers both privacy and openness. Windows are usually placed high above ground level and out of reach from the outside. The elevations are always designed from the inside, and façades are usually symmetrical. Windows can be carried down to the floor to create a place for sitting called *mandalun* or may be placed close to the ceiling to give light and air. The main façade usually contains a large number of windows (as many as fifteen) of different shapes and sizes (Ragette, 1980, p.150).

Throughout the development of different house typologies – the rectangular, gallery and *liwan* types – the rectangular window initially evolved mainly from environmental considerations, whereas in the subsequent central house typology the factors that influenced its transformation into its arched forms were mainly socio-cultural and economic (Figures 3.33a and 3.33b).

FIGURE 3.30 Balcony of gallery house with circular openings

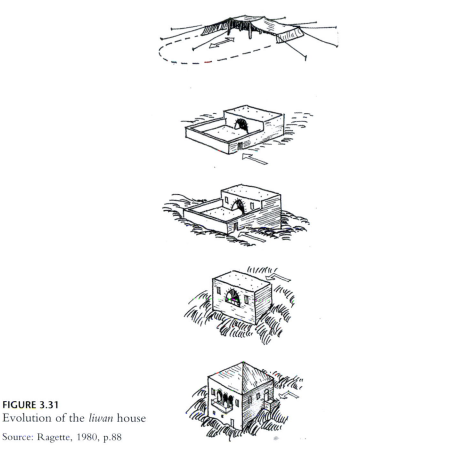

FIGURE 3.31
Evolution of the *liwan* house

Source: Ragette, 1980, p.88

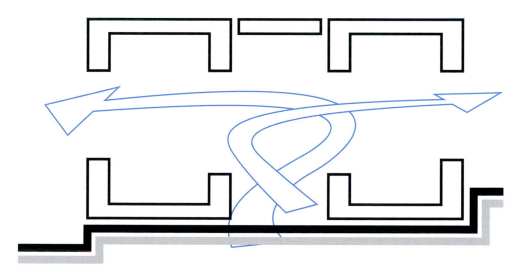

FIGURE 3.32 *Liwan* cross–ventilation

FIGURE 3.33a Central house, Keserwan

FIGURE 3.33b Central house, Sursok, Beirut

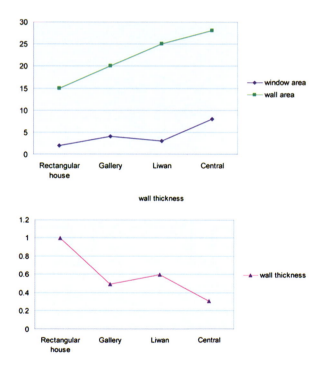

FIGURE 3.34 Window/wall ratio, comparative analysis

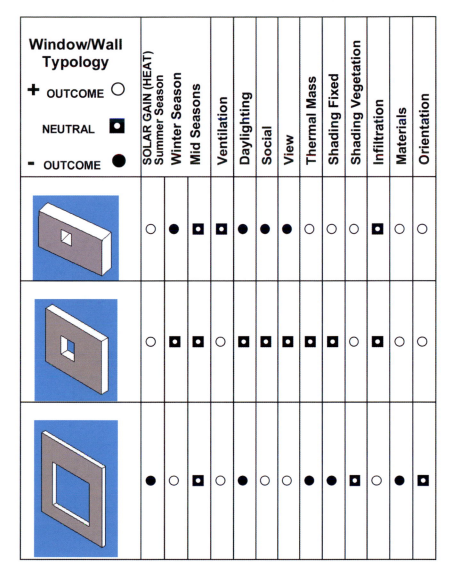

Window/Wall Typology	Solar Gain (Heat) — Summer Season	Winter Season	Mid Seasons	Ventilation	Daylighting	Social	View	Thermal Mass	Shading Fixed	Shading Vegetation	Infiltration	Materials	Orientation
(small window, thick tapered wall)	○	●	◨	◨	●	●	●	○	○	○	◨	○	○
(medium window, thick wall)	○	◨	◨	○	◨	◨	◨	◨	◨	◨	○	◨	○
(large window, thin wall)	●	○	◨	○	●	○	○	●	●	◨	○	●	◨

Legend: **+ OUTCOME** ○ **NEUTRAL** ◨ **− OUTCOME** ●

FIGURE 3.35 How variations in window size and wall thickness have affected environmental processes in Lebanese residential building

The existence of the earlier three typologies was governed by criteria that nature imposed as well as technical limitations in the building industry. Topography, solar exposure, humidity, precipitation and wind patterns were all taken into consideration (Figure 34 and Figure 3.35).

Lacking views to the outside but benefiting from massive thick walls, the basic rectangular house had the advantage of thermal inertia. In addition to maintaining a controlled interior comfort, the thick massive walls served as a shading device on windows limiting summer exposure. However, even with their limited size, the openings allowed the winter sun to enter. This was enhanced by the tapering of the wall towards the interior. This feature gradually

FIGURE 3.36 Triple arched windows, Quartier Sursok, Beirut

disappeared from the Lebanese house as view, natural ventilation and social activity gained in importance as design criteria (Figure 3.36). Larger windows increase solar gain as well as heat loss. This became very obvious when float glass came into use at the end of the nineteenth century. Auxiliary components, such as internal curtains and other shading devices, had to be used to control excessive daylighting and direct solar exposure in summer. Until then wooden shutters had been used for solar protection.

Small openings

Throughout Lebanese vernacular architecture, small openings were used for purposes that enhanced environmental strategies of natural ventilation and daylighting. Their placement was critical, especially for the winter season when shutters were commonly used to close these openings in the cooler regions (Figure 3.37). Dimensions of these small openings varied from 10×10cm to 30×50cm. The openings were placed either on the upper part of walls, above or next to windows or doors, or near ground level to draw fresh air for activities involving cooking and heating (Figure 3.38). When ventilation is not required, the lower openings are closed thus preventing undesirable air flow. The use of these openings was evidently more flexible in the original rectangular house since the walls had similar thickness, whereas the

FIGURE 3.37a Small openings, Chebaa, South Lebanon

FIGURE 3.37b Small openings (interior), Taanayel

FIGURE 3.37c Small openings (exterior), Taanayel

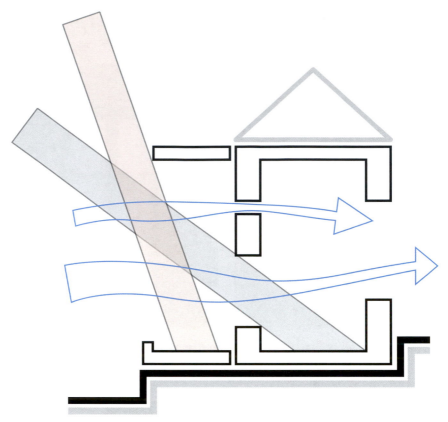

FIGURE 3.38 Cross-ventilation caused by openings

vaulted houses in all typologies restricted their use to the central part of the vaults. Within the gallery, *liwan* and central house typologies, these small openings also developed as ornamented features on the façade (see also Figure 3.30).

Triple arched window

With the turn of the twentieth century and the wide adoption of sheet glass, a trend for social expression through eclecticism began. In this period the central hall typology became the Lebanese house with the highest degree of identity. Built on a slope, it consists of two floors with a single entrance to the main floor. Its symmetrical composition includes a triple arcade. The triple arch consists of three arches connecting above slender columns, and they either tie to a wall or are supported by half columns. In some cases, this is extended to four or five arches. This combination provides a door that opens to a balcony, or a rail-protected protrusion, and windows forming a parapet. The arches were generally plain and open, until later periods when glass came into use. Wooden frames were fitted into the columns and arches with intricate designs and patterns of plain or coloured glass. Every elevation has a balcony, and thus a stronger connection to the surrounding. The new lightweight roof construction (reduction of the roof load) allowed thinner walls for the upper floors. The hall is well expressed from the façade (three arch motifs) (Ragette, 1980, p.154). The bay window, typical to Arab architecture (Figure 3.39), was more common in Islamic communities and served as a lookout for the harems. Resting upon stone corbels, the structure was mainly made of wood in a way to allow seeing without being seen (Ragette, 1980, p.157).

Pateras, rosettes and circular openings display the same creative inventiveness and embellishments observed in keystones (Figure 3.40). A special feature is the high relief design cut hollow, which is cut entirely out of one block, resembling medieval bosses. Sills vary in size (30–40cm up to 80–100cm), mainly due to the oriental habit of sitting on the floor. It later developed into what is called the *mandalun*, combining a low window with a sitting platform (Ragette, 1980, pp.150, 162).

The combination window

The combination type developed from different features of the previously stated typologies simultaneously because of three different factors: economic considerations, local conditions and personal preferences.

FIGURE 3.39a Bay window, Deir Al-Amar   **FIGURE 3.39b** Bay window, Beit El-Dine

FIGURE 3.40a, b, c, d Circular openings

Conclusion – or the present

In recent days we can no longer formulate a pattern or set guidelines for window typologies in modern Lebanese construction. The leading factors controlling the window orientation, size and shape are governmental rules and regulations that are far from being environmentally conscious. Shy attempts are being made to correct this situation by studies carried out by the United Nations Development Programme (UNDP) and building legislation authorities. Window design using modern sustainable technologies has brought flexibility to concepts of orientation, shape and size, which makes it easier to achieve required criteria. What we build defines our identity and reflects our cultural behaviour. A mere opening, one that has changed throughout history, defines how we look from it or how we are looked upon through it (Figure 3.41). As F. Ragette wrote in his book on Lebanese architecture, 'The houses of a people mirror the needs, desires and living habits of a time, because they are the direct result of the interaction between man and his environment.'

FIGURE 3.41 Old and new architecture, *ghazir*

Source: Jean Pierre Asmar, 2003

References

Corpus Levant (2004) *Rehabilitation: traditional Lebanese architecture*, Beirut, Leogravure.
Liger-Belair, Jacques (2000) *L'habitation au Liban/The Dwelling in Lebanon*, Paris, Editions Geuthner.
Ragette, Friedrich (1980) *Architecture in Lebanon*, New York, Caravan Books-Delmar.
Saliba, Robert (1998) *Beirut 1920–1940: domestic architecture between tradition and modernity*, Beirut, The Order of Engineers and Architects.
Sehnaaoui, Nada (2002) *L'occidentalisation de la Vie Quotidienne à Beyrouth: 1860–1914*, Beirut, Dar An Nahar.
UNDP (2005) 'Climate and comfort: passive design strategies for Lebanon', Project LEB/99/G35, 2005, United Nations Development Programme.

4

THE HISTORIC HAMMĀMS OF DAMASCUS AND FEZ

Magda Sibley

Introduction

Bath houses, or public baths, have existed since the Hellenistic period and flourished throughout the time of the Romans and Byzantines. Although the bathing tradition died out in the West, it continued in the Levant after the arrival of Muslim Arabs. The period following the rise of Islam witnessed a rapid development in the history of public baths and a change from Roman to Islamic bathing habits. A process of assimilation of the Roman and Byzantine baths

MAP 4 Damascus, Syria

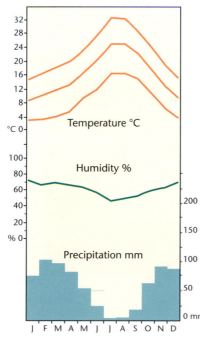

GRAPH 4A Fes, Morocco

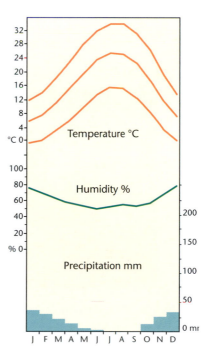

GRAPH 4B Damascus, Syria

has taken place, during which features that responded to the needs, traditions and religious beliefs were retained while others were discarded.

During the first century of the Islamic calendar (AD 622) there was a wide spread of Roman baths with a three-room composition (frigidarium, tepidarium and calidarium), and the first Islamic hammāms consisted of a linear progression of rooms with varying temperatures. The most well-known surviving example is Qusayr Amra in the Jordanian Desert (Figure 4.1).

The religious requirements for washing in Islam played an important role in the way hammāms developed. For example, the cold plunge pool, a major feature of the Roman baths, disappeared in the Islamic baths. Although pools existed in some hammāms of Palestine and Greater Syria, bathing by immersion was not common during the Islamic period as it was considered inappropriate. Instead, bathing in running water became the norm. The Islamic public bath forms part of the triad of essential urban facilities in the Islamic city – the mosque, the hammām and the suq. It is an urban facility that not only facilitates the accomplishment of the great ablutions (hence its location near mosques) but also plays an important social function as it serves as a meeting place for both male and female society. Despite the importance of this building type, the hammām as an institution has been in decline since the nineteenth century, particularly with the introduction of private bathroom facilities in modern housing. Many hammāms have closed, have fallen into disrepair or have been completely destroyed. The rate at which evidence of this important building type is being removed is alarming, particularly as this building type presents unique lessons of environmental, social and economical sustainability.

This chapter is based on surveys carried out by the author on the hammāms of Fez and Damascus in 2000 and 2004 respectively. The work was carried out as part of research projects funded by the Arts and Humanities Research Board (now Research Council) in the UK. The chapter presents the main characteristics of this building type as studied in two world heritage cities located in distinct geographical areas. In 2006, as part of an EU-funded research project, the hammāms of Fez and Damascus were again visited by the author, establishing a clear picture of the different conditions in which they survive and operate in the twenty-first century.

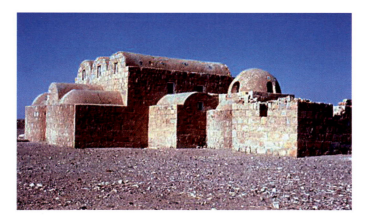

FIGURE 4.1 Qusayr Amra: early Umayyad bath built between 712 and 715

Source: www.archnet.org/library

The public baths of Fez

Studies on hammāms in North Africa and the Middle East are few and far between. Edmund Pauty (Pauty, 1933) made an extensive survey of the hammāms in Cairo in the 1930s. Slightly later Claude Ecochard and Michel Le Coeur published a major reference work on the hammāms of Damascus (Ecochard and Le Coeur, 1942/1943). In Morocco, most published surveys date back to the French Protectorate period (1912–1957). The work of Henri Terrasse (Terrasse, 1950) analyses three Merinide hammāms, and the work of Edmond Secret (Secret, 1942 and 1990) concentrates on surveying the hammāms in Fez. More recently – in the 1990s – a survey was carried out on the Islamic baths in Palestine (Dow, 1992).

The majority of historic hammāms in the medina of Fez have managed to survive and continue to function today. This is mainly due to the fact that the medina of Fez has managed to survive in its integrity and is still inhabited today. The peripheral location of the Maghreb shielded it from major geographical conflicts that hit the Fertile Crescent and Egypt, such as the crusades and the two waves of Mongol invasions leading to the destruction of earlier historic structures. When Morocco fell under the French protectorate in 1912, the colonial city of Fez was established away from the historic urban fabric. These factors played an important role in the preservation of the urban integrity of the medina of Fez and its traditional urban facilities such as the hammāms. The prosperity of Fez during the rule of various dynasties was expressed in the number of public baths that the city enjoyed. It was estimated that ninety-three hammāms existed in Fez during the Almohades period in the twelfth century. During the Merinide dynasty, established in 1248, Fez acquired the status of a capital and continued to flourish, as did its public baths. In 1999–2000, thirty historic hammāms were still operating and half of them were visited by the author. In 2006 most of these baths were still operating although some had closed down because of financial difficulties and/or the deterioration of the building fabric due to the lack of proper maintenance. It is important to note that these historic hammāms are still providing an important urban facility for a poor population living in overcrowded conditions in the deteriorating old courtyard houses where multi-family occupation is the norm and where bathroom facilities are not available to all.

Urban location and water distribution system

The old city of Fez is situated in a bowl with a plateau above it receiving the river of Fez. The traditional water distribution system was based on the gravity system whereby the river was divided at the top plateau into various underground channels that descended to the different quarters of the Medina. The hammāms are located along the underground water channels and are built on sloping sites to help with water drainage. Some hammāms are located next to existing natural springs or wells and offer a public fountain. This is the case for hammāms Moulay Idriss and Seffarine in Fez. The location and frequency of the hammāms depended also on their proximity to large mosques, commercial districts (or *suks*) or neighbourhood centres.

Hammāms are generally well embedded in the traditional urban fabric of the city. Their position is never prominent, their entrance is discreet, and their façades are totally blind. Their presence in the urban fabric is more evident at roof level because of the pierced domes and vaults that are specific to them and are not found in any other building type (Figure 4.2).

FIGURE 4.2 Hammām Seffarine in Fez evident by its roof domes

Form and function

Islamic baths are much smaller than the Roman baths and more frequent within the urban fabric. They are never free-standing structures but are surrounded by other buildings, reducing the area of their exposed external walls to that of the entrance façade only.

The form and function of the hammām in Fez has remained constant from medieval times onwards. While the Mamluk and Ottoman public baths in Damascus tend to have a central organization of the bathing spaces, the hammāms surveyed in Fez have maintained a linear and axial organization reminiscent of the first Umayyad public baths. They all follow the same configuration of four sequential rooms: *Mashlah* or *Goulsa* – the Roman apodyterium; *al-Barrani* – the Roman frigidarium; *al-Wastani* – the Roman tepidarium; and *al-Dakhli* – the Roman caldarium. This is illustrated in the plans and sections of hammām Seffarine (Figure 4.3a), one of the most well-known hammāms in Fez, located near the main religious centre of the Qaraouyyine mosque and hammām Mekhfia (Figure 4.3b) known for its beautiful war room dome.

The undressing/dressing room is usually accessed from the street through a bent entrance, which prevents visual intrusion into the internal spaces. This room is usually covered with a high dome and is the largest and most decorated space in the hammāms of Fez. It usually displays a beautiful fountain built against the wall separating the undressing room and the bathing spaces and has beautiful carved stucco and cedar wood decorations. The walls are covered halfway down by finely coloured locally produced ceramic tiles locally known as *zellidj*. The changing areas are slightly raised from the centre of the room and consist of seating and lockers along the peripheral walls of the undressing space. The reception area is located within the same space, next to the entrance of the hammām. The access to the cold room is through an intermediate corridor where toilets are located. Next is the first room or *barrani*, which consists of a small space used by clients to rest from the heat of the warm and the hot rooms. The next space is the *wasti* or warm room and is usually the largest and main bathing

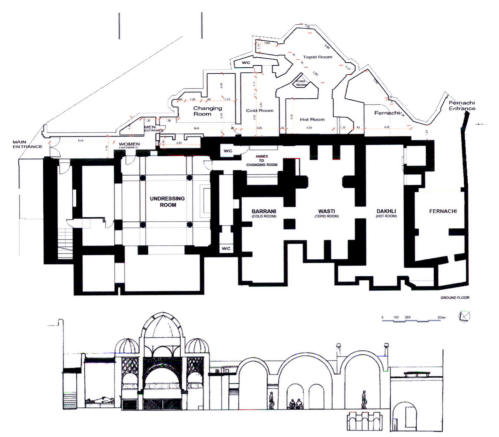

FIGURE 4.3a Hammām Seffarine floor plan and section

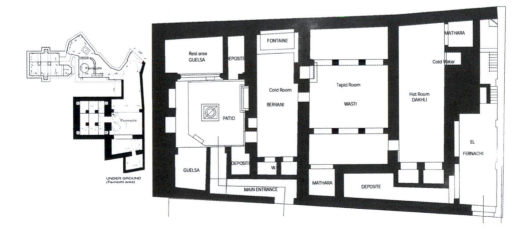

FIGURE 4.3b Hammām Mekhfia floor plan and section

space covered by a pierced dome or vault. Unlike the hammāms of Damascus, there are no pipes in the walls circulating hot and cold water, and no individual stone washing basins to receive the water. Buckets of hot and cold water are filled from the hot water pool in the hot room and from the cold water pool in the cold room respectively. These are placed in the warm room and hot and cold water is mixed for the required temperature. The water is scooped from the buckets by a small brass bowl called a *tassa*. Traditionally, water was collected from the hot water pool using a wooden bucket called the *kebb*, which has a capacity of twenty litres. The amount of water each client received was in the past limited to four to six wooden buckets – anything above this quantity had to be paid for. Plastic buckets have now replaced the traditional wooden ones, although these are still being made in the medina. The final room, the hot room or *dakhli*, is adjacent to the furnace and contains a large basin of hot water locally called *burma*. The hot water arrives directly from the cauldrons placed in the furnace, releasing steam into the space.

The heating system

The heating section of the hammām – the furnace or *furnatchi* – is built against one of the walls of the hot room. It has its own entrance for the delivery of the fuel and has no access to the bathing spaces. The furnace is sometimes combined with a public bakery to make economic use of the furnace and the firewood. The furnace (*furnatchi*) presents a small lodge for the attendant (*sahan*) and, sometimes, a stable for the donkeys used for delivering the fuel, which usually consists of recycled materials such as wood shavings and olive pits that are dumped in heaps in the furnace. The fire is lit under two or more large brass cauldrons measuring two metres in diameter and three to four metres in height. These cauldrons are locally made in the neighbouring Seffarine square. The warm and hot rooms are heated using the hypocaust system traditionally used in the Roman baths (Figure 4.4). The hot smoke travels beneath the floor, which is suspended on brick pillars, and is then expelled through the chimneys embedded in the four corners of the hot room.

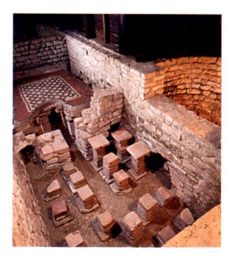

FIGURE 4.4 The ancient Roman hypocaust system

Source: www.wikipedia.org, section on hypocaust

The heating system is a labour-intensive device as it requires constant attention to feed the fire and remove the ashes. The *furnatchi* attendant works from four o'clock in the morning until 10 o'clock at night, keeping the furnace fire going by throwing fuel into the furnace on a regular basis (Figure. 4.5). All the *furnatchis* visited in 2000 and in 2006 in the Medina of Fez were still operating in the traditional way. The fuel is still transported to the hammāms on donkeys' backs and dumped in heaps in the *furnatchi*. The majority of the visited hammāms are equipped with four chimneys. They are connected directly to furnace and to the hypocaust. Smoke pollution is generally a problem for the neighbouring houses and some hammāms such as Moulay Idriss and Boussouifa have a water filter system connected directly to the chimneys in order to help reduce pollution from the smoke.

In terms of energy consumption, hammāms consume large quantities of fuel wood. It was estimated in 2007 that biomass energy consumption by hammāms was 430,000 tonnes per year. Considering that nationwide there are 2400 hammāms in Morocco, improving the energy efficiency of their heating boilers could have a significant impact on reducing deforestation and environmental pollution. However, this should also be combined with an appropriate design and construction of the building as it was noticed that unlike the historic ones, which have a high thermal mass and are designed to retain the heat, the new ones are generally of a very poor construction and thermal performance.

Social customs and habits

The vast majority of the historic public baths of Fez consist of a single hammām, i.e. they do not have two separate sections for men and women but operate different schedules for them. They allow for the easy accomplishment of the great ablution and for maintaining

FIGURE 4.5a The furnace space

FIGURE 4.5b Delivery of fuel in Hammām Mekhfia

cleanliness and health for a poor population. Furthermore, the hammām forms an important part of the lives of Moroccan women and is associated with the celebration of important life events such as weddings, the birth of a child and circumcision. A number of customs, traditions and rituals have been transmitted from one generation to another and are still alive today. Some hammāms are associated with a religious figure, for which an alcove is allocated in the hot room and where women light candles as prayers. Hammāms have also sustained a number of social practices that are very much alive and represent a rich non-tangible element of urban heritage. In addition to cleanliness and beauty treatment, steam baths provide a number of health benefits in terms of reducing muscle tension and stress, improving the circulation of blood near the skin and eliminating toxins through perspiration.

It was evident during the field work that the historic hammāms in Fez have sustained their function up to the present day. This can be explained by the fact that they are still very much needed by the local poor population living in the various historic quarters of the medina, with a multi-family occupancy of the traditional courtyard houses where contemporary bathroom facilities are not available for each family.

Current situation and lessons for the future

It is important to note that the social practice of going to the hammām is still very much alive in Morocco. Such a practice is not limited to the poor population of the medina, as new public baths are being built in new neighbourhoods where dwelling units have their own private bathroom facilities. It is interesting to note that the new hammāms tend to reproduce the traditional spatial organization; however, their construction method and their new heating systems are far from being environmentally efficient. Furthermore, there are no general guidelines about their design and construction. Private steam baths are also being built in large villas and hotels, and their benefits are widely acknowledged today.

Most historic hammāms are suffering from poor maintenance or a total lack of it, resulting in a continuous deterioration of their building fabric. Their roofs seem to be the main source of problems, with poor rain water drainage, extensions and additions of cold water tanks, and the deterioration of the glass bulbs located on the domes and the vaults. Furthermore, the internal spaces are subject to insensitive transformations ranging from incompatible floor and wall finishes to spatial subdivisions. None of the hammāms of Fez is registered as a heritage building and none has ever been the focus of any conservation, restoration and rehabilitation project. Direct observation revealed that some of the historic structures are in danger of collapse, particularly in the furnace area. In some cases, domes have collapsed and have been replaced by reinforced flat concrete slabs that lack the thermal characteristics of the original construction. A number of other insensitive alterations have taken place, particularly in the entrance and reception areas. There is a need for these structures to be considered as heritage buildings that deserve urgent safeguarding and rehabilitation.

The public baths of Damascus

A survey of the public baths of Damascus was conducted by the author in 2004, and this provided an updated list of the historic public baths of Damascus and their condition and usage in the twenty-first century. Of the forty operating hammāms identified in the 1940s (Ecochard and Le Coeur, 1942/1943) only thirteen were still operating in 2004; the remainder had either been demolished or had changed function (Sibley, 2007). It is clear that the rate at which this building type is disappearing in Damascus is alarming. The few surviving examples are usually located within the walled city and are near major commercial or tourist areas.

The evolution of the hammāms of Damascus

Unlike the public baths of Fez, which have retained the early configuration of the first Islamic baths, those in Damascus have evolved and changed over the centuries. Ecochard and Le Coeur produced the most comprehensive record of the historic public baths of Damascus. Detailed drawings were produced for twenty-nine hammāms dating from the fourteenth century to the nineteenth century (Ecochard and Le Coeur, 1942/1943). A careful analysis of their layout was carried out, highlighting a slow evolution of their internal organization. They have evolved away from the Roman baths: the bathing spaces in general and the hot room in particular have become dominant over the other spaces. The proportions of the bathing spaces and their arrangements have also witnessed variations throughout different historic periods. It is evident that the hot room developed over the centuries at the expense of the other washing rooms and became the only washing space in the nineteenth century (Figure 4.6). Whereas the pre-Ottoman hammāms displayed a clear sequence of warm and hot room, with associated side chambers, the Ottoman baths consist mainly of a simple hot room and side chambers. It is important to note that in the case of the hammāms of Fez, the warm room has remained the main bathing space.

In addition to the changes in the importance and proportions of the bathing spaces, their spatial organization has also seen various developments. Two typical organizations can be found in the pre-fourteenth century hammāms: a sequential, linear one where the bathing spaces are organized along an axis and a central one where the spaces are organized around a main octagonal room. Both types of organizations co-existed simultaneously between the twelfth and fourteenth centuries, after which only the central organization remained until the eighteenth century when the internal organization went back to a linear organization with a loss of complex architectural forms (Figure 4.6).

The co-existence of both linear and central organizations within the same city in the twelfth and thirteenth centuries can be explained by the existence of two sources of influences in the antiquity. The octagonal compositions with diagonal extensions of bathing spaces are reminiscent of Byzantine architecture whereas the linear organization is reminiscent of the early Umayyad baths (Figures 4.7 and 4.8).

Form and function

As in the case of Fez, a typical hammām in Damascus consists of two activity areas: the undressing room or rooms (*Meshlah*) and the washing areas (*al-Berrani, al-Westani* and *al-Dakhli*). The undressing room is usually the largest space covered by a dome and has raised stone benches (*or mastabas*) around the walls. All the hammāms of Damascus have a central water feature in their undressing room and their washing areas contain stone or marble washing basins (*jurns*) receiving hot and cold water from clay pipes embedded in the walls. The hot room or *bayt-al-nar* is the bathing space adjacent to the furnace. The furnace or *qammīm* is built against the hot room. The fire is lit under two or more large brass cauldrons built into the furnace, and the whole of the upper furnace serves as water reservoir.

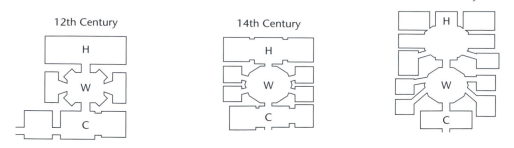

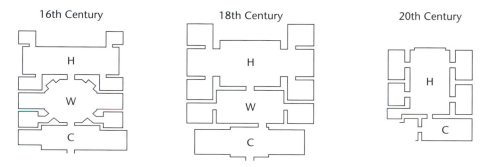

H: Hot room   W: Warm room   C: Cold room

FIGURE 4.6 Evolution of the hammām layout in Damascus between the twelfth century and the nineteenth century

Source: Adapted from Ecochard and Le Coeur, 1942/1943

The duct heating system

Whereas the hammāms of Fez maintained the heating system of the early Umayyad baths (a hypocaust system inherited from Roman and Byzantine times), the heating system of the medieval hammāms of Damascus consists of a smoke duct travelling under the floor of the washing rooms (Figure 4.7b). The smoke from the fire in the furnace passes along a duct under the floor of the hot room and rises up in a chimney in the wall separating the warm room from the cold one. The duct branches out into the side chambers and its presence with its branches is made evident by the way the floor paving changes from a pink stone to a black basalt stone tiling. The floor over the duct is known as the fire slab or *bilāt al-nār*. The furnace is kept working late at night, allowing the structure to remain warm. Unfortunately all the surviving and working historic hammāms of Damascus have abandoned the traditional heating system and replaced it by a boiler fuelled by diesel. Concerns about air pollution and pressure from local authorities have led to this change of heating system. There is, however, one exception, and that is hammām Ammuna located outside the city walls and this hammām continues to recycle wood shavings and garbage as fuel for its furnace with the use of the under-floor duct heating system.

It is clear that the replacement of the heating system by a boiler is not necessarily environmentally friendly. Furthermore, the under-floor heating system that allowed for the

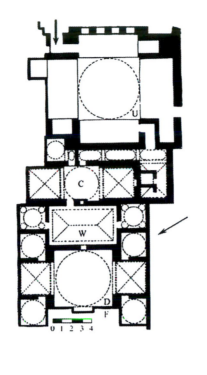

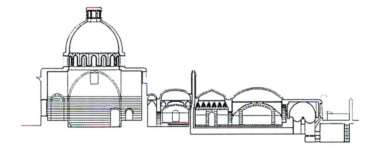

FIGURE 4.7 Plan and section of hammām Ammuneh (fourteenth century) showing its linear
organisation and the underfloor duct heating system

Source: Adapted from Ecochard and le Coeur, 1942/1943

spaces to maintain comfortable warm temperature has been completely abandoned. The rooms
are heated by allowing steam from the boiler to enter the bathing spaces, but when the boiler
is stopped during the night, the bathing spaces and the building fabric cool down rapidly and
take more time to heat again the next day.

Natural lighting and ventilation: the pierced domes and vaults

The most distinctive feature of the hammāms is the way the domes and vaults over the washing
rooms are pierced with circular or star-shaped roof lights, forming intricate patterns. Whereas

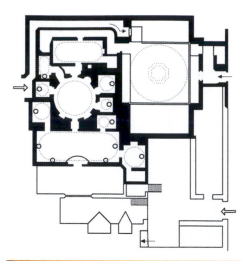

FIGURE 4.8 *(Top left and right)* Hammām al Tayrouzi, Damascus (sixteenth century). a) Central organisation of bathing spaces; b) Roof architecture of the bathing spaces with pierced domes and vaults

Source: Adapted from Ecochard and le Coeur, 1942/1943, p.66

FIGURE 4.9 *(Left and below)* Roof openings. a) Geometric patterns of *qamariyyats* in hammām Ammuneh; b) Pierced domes and vaults in hammām Fethi, Damascus (eighteenth century)

Roman and Byzantine bathhouses are naturally lit with a central lantern at the top of the dome and windows placed at the lower edge of the dome, the Islamic bath houses are characterized by multiple circular or star-shaped openings over the whole surface of the dome and closed by glass caps. These openings consist of pottery tubes built into the domes, closed by glass covers and arranged according to various decorative geometric patterns, and are locally called *qamariyyat* (Figure 4.9). Some of these glass bulbs are removable in order to allow for natural ventilation to take place when the bathing spaces are not used. These architectural features can be found as early as the seventh century as evidenced in Qusayr Amra. They allow for daylight to enter the bathing spaces and create a special atmosphere enhanced by the high concentration of steam in the bathing spaces.

Construction systems

One of the main requirements of the building envelope is to have a high level of thermal mass in order to keep the heat in. The walls are traditionally of a thick stone or brick construction and the domes and vaults are built with bricks. The floors are tiled with stone or marble or with ceramic tiles as is the case in Morocco. Special waterproof renders and plasters are made from a lime mortar to which ashes from the furnace are added. In the case of Fez, egg yolks are added to lime plasters in order to provide a smooth waterproof finish to the walls. The walls of all bathing spaces in the hammāms of Damascus were traditionally rendered. Render was applied directly on the rabble-stone structure in two coats. The first coat was meant for smoothing the surface and therefore its thickness could vary; the second coat was about 4–5 mm thick. The original render consisted of slaked lime from the quarries of Qasyoun, hemp grown in the Ghouta grounds, and plaster obtained from gypsum extracted at Jeroud. According to textual sources, the walls of the warm and cold rooms were sometimes covered halfway down (up to one metre) with a red-coloured coating, obtained by mixing grounded brick to the render (Ecochard and Le Coeur, 1942/1943, I, p.39). The washing basins located in the warm and hot rooms, as well as in the *maqsoura*, were carved in a solid stone piece. The floor of all bathing spaces was covered by polychromatic stones and marble tiles arranged according to more or less complex geometrical patterns. The majority of the tiling consisted of alternate stripes of black basalt and pink limestone from the quarries of Mezze. Because of the high thermal conductivity values of basalt, it was used for covering the under-floor passage of the heating duct, which was thus marked by a wide black stripe running along the bathing spaces up to the intermediate room.

Current usage and transformations

Unlike Morocco, the tradition of going to the hammām is disappearing in Syria and the Middle East. There are no new hammāms being built in new residential areas and many of the historic ones are used as storage spaces or workshops. The few surviving ones are struggling to continue as the rising cost of water, fuel and personnel are making them uneconomical to run. Those located near the touristic historic areas have been restored and have introduced new functions such as massage rooms, showers and a pool as well as a hairdresser/barber and a café in the main changing area. Most of those still operating in the residential neighbourhoods have ceased to open for women, contributing to the disappearance of a rich intangible heritage associated with their usage by women. However, the work conducted by the HAMMAM project consortium in hammām Ammuneh and its neighbourhood in February 2007 has contributed in raising local awareness about the heritage value of this building type and its important role in providing a social meeting place for relaxation, particularly for women. The hammām has been saved from closure and has been bought by a private client who has restored it and re-opened it as neighbourhood hammām with additional new facilities for women.

Future developments

It is clear that the hammām as a traditional building type offers a number of lessons of sustainability in terms of construction, heating system, water use and management, cleanliness, well being, and social and economic sustainability. Although there are clear regional variations in terms of contemporary usages and perceptions of these facilities as one moves from the Middle East to North Africa, there are common opportunities that can be developed based on water storage and management (in countries where water cuts are frequent) and the use of solar energy at the scale of a neighbourhood. The hammām as a building type could be reinterpreted for the development of a new urban facility that can be easily built in tight urban infill plots, making good use of derelict urban sites. They could provide an essential facility for women and children, which in addition to the washing and beauty treatment functions could combine with other functions such health awareness, education, recreation and social gatherings and recycling. There is, however, a need to develop new guidelines for both the restoration of historic hammām structures and the construction of new ones. Those guidelines should be based not only on the various lessons the historic hammāms present in terms of architecture, construction technique and space and water heating systems, but also on the new health and safety regulations and new building technologies that can be appropriately applied to this building type.

References

Dow, M. (1992) *The Islamic baths of Palestine*, Jerusalem, The British School of Archaeology in Jerusalem.

Ecochard, M. and Le Coeur, C. (1942/1943) *Les bains de Damas I and II*, Beirut, Institut Francais de Damas.

Pauty, E. (1933) *Les hammāms du Caire*, Cairo, IFAO.

Secret, E. (1942) 'Les Hammāms de Fez', *Bulletin de L'institut d'hygiene du Maroc*, Nov. Serie, 1/11/1942, pp.61–77.

Secret, E. (1990) 'Les Hammams de Fès', in E. Secret, *Les Sept Printemps de Fès*, Tours, Impression Aps., pp.57–67.

Sibley, M. (2007) 'The Pre-Ottoman public baths of Damascus and their survival into the 21st century: an analytical survey', *Journal of Architectural and Planning Research*, vol. 24, no. 4, pp.271–288.

Terrasse, H. (1950) 'Trois bains mérinides du Maroc', in *Mélanges offerts à William Marçais par l'Institut d'Études Islamiques de l'Université de Paris*, Paris, Éditions G.-P, Maisonneuve, pp.311–320.

5

CLIMATIC DESIGN OF ISLAMIC BATH BUILDINGS

Jean Bouillot

MAP 5 Cairo, Egypt

Introduction

The hammām Bab El Bahr, situated close to the north limit of the old city of Cairo, was selected as a case study introducing the environmental design features and attributes of this building type. The building was built during the Ottoman period, probably during the nineteenth century, reusing some pre-existing building elements, including some columns and capitals. Built at the corner of a handicraft-shopping street with a connection alley (Figure 5.1), it was an important facility for the neighbourhood before the surrounding houses had their own water supply and private bathrooms. The hammām itself is now also connected to the city's water supply system, and its steam producing equipment has been converted to run on oil. Though still functioning, the building is in poor condition owing to lack of maintenance. However, even in its poor current condition the building has revealed worthwhile design qualities that should ensure its restoration and continued use.

Building survey

The field study at the hammām Bab El Bahr included measurements taken over a twenty-four-hour period (Figure 5.2). The equipment was placed on the manager's desk (R1). Three sensors were positioned in specific places inside the hammām avoiding contact with walls and positioned some 1.50m above floor level. These were

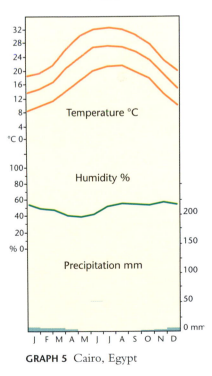

GRAPH 5 Cairo, Egypt

FIGURE 5.1 Sharia Bab el Bahr and on the left the hammām entrance

in the resting room (S2), the warm room (S3) and in the steam room (S4). A fifth sensor was placed in the corner shop in Sharia Bab el Bahr (S5), to record the maximum and minimum outdoor air temperature and relative humidity. The readings are summarized in Table 5.1 and are also plotted on the building bioclimatic chart (1 and 3) of Cairo where the thermal comfort zone and its potential extensions as well as weather data for March are also shown (Figure 5.3). The following observations can be drawn from the readings:

- 'Climate zone 3' at the entrance lobby was within comfort range most of the time (Figure 5.3).
- 'Climate zone 4' in the hot steam room ranged between 31°C and 35°C in temperature and very high relative humidity.
- The temperature in the resting room is close to that at the entrance lobby and thus too low for those returning from the warm hall (Figure 5.4).
- Over the twenty-four hours the temperature difference between 'climate zone 4' (warm room) and 'climate zone 3' (rest room) varied by 3–10°C, an average of over 5°C.
- At the time of the measurements the street microclimate outside the building (as recorded for this case study) was milder than that of the city (as recorded by the local meteorological station), being less dry (by about 10 per cent) and warmer (higher mean minimum temperature by about 11°C, as well as higher mean maximum temperature by 1.5°C), the effect of shading and heat storage by the surrounding building masses.
- The measurements showed that indoor environmental conditions in the hammām varied with its alternating use by male and female clients.

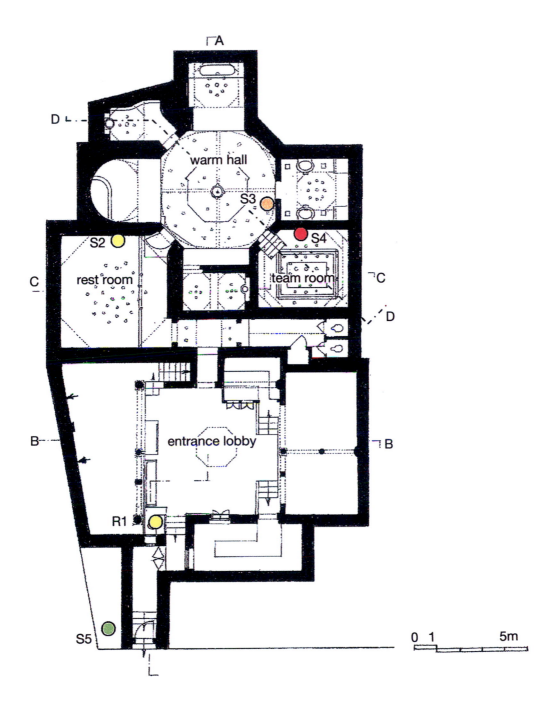

FIGURE 5.2 Plan of hammām Bab el Bahr in Cairo and five sensor positions

TABLE 5.1 Summary of temperature and humidity measurements

Days	Hours	Data	R1 (climate 3) entrance lobby	S2 3' rest room	S3 4' warm room	S4 (climate 4) steam room	S5 (climate 2) street
Wednesday 1 March	6:00 pm	T°	22°C	25.7°C	29°C	33.4°C	
		H°	62 %	72%	94%	95%	
	7:00 pm	T°	23°C	23.6°C	29.3°C	33.9°C	
		H°	62 %	73%	97%	97%	
	11:00 pm	T°	23°C	23.8°C	30.3°C	34.1°C	
		H°	64 %	84%	100%	100%	
Thursday 2 March	1:00 am	T°	23°C	24°C	34°C	34°C	
		H°	61 %	88%	100%	100%	
	3:00 am	T°	24°C	23.8°C	28.9°C	33.5°C	
		H°	61 %	87%	100%	100%	
	5:00 am	T°	25°C	24°C	28.7°C	33°C	
		H°	62 %	89%	100%	100%	
	7:00 am	T°	25°C	23°C	28.4°C	32.7°C	17.5°C
		H°	65 %	85%	100%	100%	57%
	8:00 am	T°	23°C	23.1°C	28.4°C	32.3°C	
		H°	61 %	81%	100%	100%	
	9:00 am	T°	21°C	23.3°C	27.5°C	32.2°C	
		H°	60 %	79%	100%	100%	
	11:00 am	T°	22°C	23.3°C	28.6°C	33°C	
		H°	61 %	81%	100%	100%	
	5:00 pm	T°	22°C	24.3°C	28°C	31.5°C	25.7°C
		H°	61 %	100%	100%	100%	38%
	7:00 pm	T°	22°C	23.1°C	28.4°C	31.9°C	
		H°	60 %	81%	100%	100%	

The environmental role of the architecture

The question arises of how the architecture of this building affected its environmental performance. Although a small amount of heat is contributed to the entrance lobby each time the door opens from the warm hall and the resting room, some half of the building's spaces, including the access corridor, entrance lobby, changing rooms and rest areas, work passively. One feature of the building that may be contributing to this is the ground contact provided by the lowered lobby floor, which is 1.50m below grade (Figure 5.5, e.l.) and the warm hall, which is 1.90m (Figure 5.5, w.h.) below street level. Combined with the thickness of the masonry walls, the surrounding soil contributes to the building's thermal inertia providing the heat storage required in both winter and summer. A second feature is the change in floor levels and room heights within the building and their effects on air flow and stratification (Figure 5.6). Lowering of the floor retains the cooler air, whereas the heat stratifies toward the raised ceiling of the central area, providing the hammmām staff with a place to hang

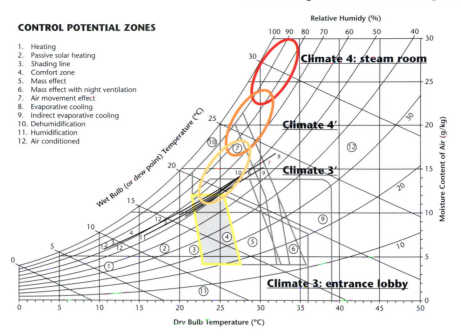

FIGURE 5.3 Building bio-climatic chart of Beirut–Tripoli with conjectural hammām micro–climates from climate 3 to climate 4 and two transitional climates 3' and 4'

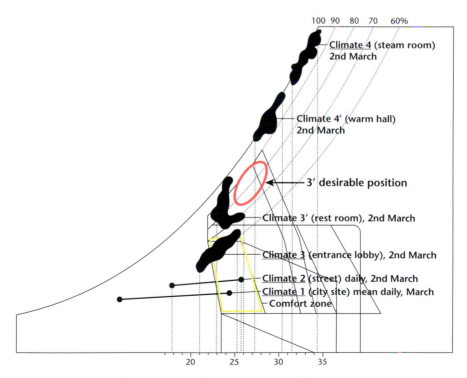

FIGURE 5.4 Psychometric chart showing the microclimates of the Cairo hammām

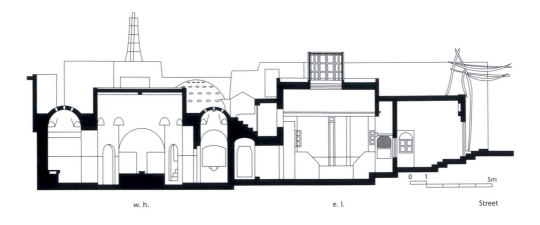

w. h.   e. l.   Street

FIGURE 5.5 Longitudinal section AA

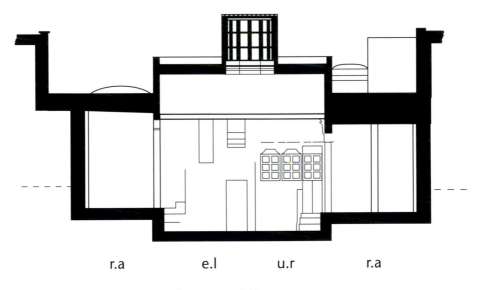

r.a   e.l   u.r   r.a

FIGURE 5.6 Cross-section through the entrance lobby

towels to dry in winter; in summer, opening the upper lantern and the door to the terrace promotes air movements that dry the towels.

Even if the heated area of the hammām requires mechanical systems, the same passive devices are at work there as well and help to save energy: the thermal coupling with the ground, the air stratification and the high-inertia construction. In the steam room (Figure 5.7), which is situated 1.47m above the warm hall, the heat and steam rising from the warm pool ascend towards the dome over this space and stay trapped there, thus maintained inside. Like an upside-down bottle, the warmth and steam may flow toward the warm room only

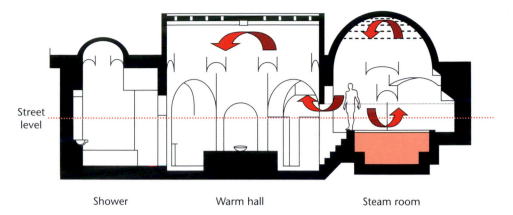

Street level

Shower

Warm hall

Steam room

FIGURE 5.7 Cross section DD through the steam room and warm hall

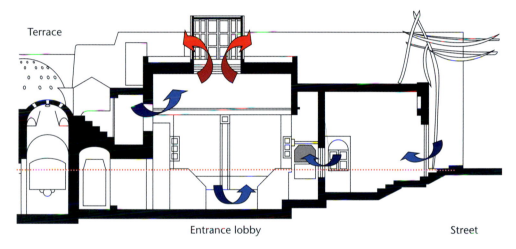

Terrace

Entrance lobby

Street

FIGURE 5.8 Summer night and ventilation system in the entrance lobby

when the dome has filled up, but the higher temperatures are always experienced in the steam room owing to air stratification.

The seasonal adaptation of the passive area requires minimal manipulation. During winter all the outside openings are closed; these include the double door in the entrance corridor, the window in the manager's space, the door to the terrace and the upper lantern. Warmth from the heated areas and metabolic heat gains in conjunction with the thermal inertia of the building contribute to stable temperatures. In summer (Figure 5.8), the building openings must be kept closed during daytime to prevent hot air penetration from outside, except for the lantern, which helps exhaust residual heat, provided that no solar radiation is admitted into the lobby. Outside in the street the canopy shades the entrance of the hammām. At night the terrace access door, the entrance corridor the window of the manager's desk and the lantern will be opened in order to promote a continuous air circulation to cool the structure and exhaust the warm air to the outside.

The building structure is a mixture of masonry and timber elements. Walls are of stone held with lime mortar, pouzzolane lime and multi-layer plastering in the inferior parts and brickwork with pouzzolane lime mortar with flat roofs on timber structure. In the actively controlled areas, the structure is of masonry construction and brickwork for the dome with its many small glazed openings.

Conclusion

The connection between the architecture and the environmental performance of the building is real. Even if the heating equipment is required to produce heat and steam, the building design allows for its efficient use and distribution to the hammām's different microclimates.

Acknowledgement

This paper was made possible by the EC 'HAMMAM' Project, 'Hammam, Aspects and Multidisciplinary Methods of Analysis for the Mediterranean region'.

6

THE ENVIRONMENTAL PERFORMANCE OF A TRADITIONAL COURTYARD HOUSE IN CHINA

Benson Lau, Brian Ford and Zhang Hongru

MAP 6 Zhouzhuang, China

Introduction

The fishing village of Zhouzhuang is in south-east China, about 30km south-east of Suzhou and west of Shanghai, located at the junction of the lakes of Baixian and Beibai. Zhouzhuang has remained a village of natural beauty and tranquillity for many centuries, and has survived remarkably intact.

In Zhouzhuang, nearly 1000 households are distributed along the canals, streets and lanes. Most of the original architecture is preserved, including almost one hundred ancient houses with courtyards and sixty carved brick archways (Chen Yi et al., 2000). With white walls and lattice windows, the residential houses are located close to the rivers and lakes, manifesting a tranquil and picturesque atmosphere (Figure 6.1).

Founded as a Buddhist monastery in the eleventh century, it has an economy based initially on the abundant aquatic life of the lakes, though it later became a centre of grain, silk and art and craft production. The settlement grew around a network of natural and man-made waterways, in a similar way (but on a smaller scale) to Souzhou, which has a worldwide reputation for its exquisite 'Scholar Gardens'.

Within Zhouzhuang, many of the buildings date back to the Ming and Qiang Dynasties. This study focuses on one particular house, and the subtlety of the ways in

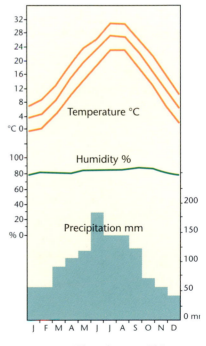

GRAPH 6 Zhouzhuang, China

FIGURE 6.1 The fishing village, Zhouzhuang

which it was designed to respond to seasonal changes in climate, to achieve not just visual and thermal comfort throughout the year, but also a calm and dignified interior that delights all the senses (Figure 6.2).

Climatic conditions

Zhouzhuang has a subtropical monsoon climate with four distinct seasons. The summer months are hot and humid with an average temperature of 26°C, while the winter months are cold and humid with an average temperature of 6°C. The annual average temperature is about 16°C and the relative humidity varies from 30 percent to 80 per cent.

South-easterly winds characterize the warm season, thus bringing warmth and high humidity from the ocean, as well as monsoon rain for part of the season. North-westerly polar winds bringing cold and damp characterize the cold season.

Zhang's house and the 'crab eye' light wells

The entrance to Zhang's house faces almost due west, adjacent to a landing stage from the canal (Figure 6.3). It is the private residence of a wealthy merchant, and follows the traditional layout of public reception and ceremonial halls in the front with more private living spaces for the family behind (this layout is commonly found in the private residence in China, although most houses were positioned on a strict north/south axis).

FIGURE 6.2 Zhang's house: view of ceremonial hall

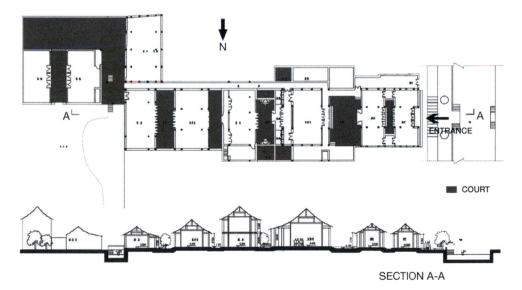

SECTION A-A

FIGURE 6.3 Zhang's house: ground floor plan and section

Frontage to the river/canal would have been very valuable, so the houses have a relatively narrow frontage and are stretched out as a series of pavilions and courts, the geometry of which is manipulated to provide light and air while maintaining privacy and security.

From the first low reception hall, the contemporary visitor is allowed to proceed directly on axis via a very narrow (2m wide) court into a second reception hall, from where one looks through a very imposing doorway within a blank masonry wall, towards a slightly raised and much bigger ceremonial hall, which is reached across a larger courtyard (Figure 6.4).

In the past, the central screen doors between the reception pavilions may have generally been closed (except in summer to allow air movement), and the visitor would have been forced to go either side of the first narrow court, not gaining a glimpse of the ceremonial hall until arriving at the imposing central doorway.

The door here is heavy and solid and sits within a completely opaque masonry wall, not allowing light or air to pass through, and providing a line of security and privacy. Standing just inside this doorway, one has a clear view of the imposing ceremonial hall opposite, and

FIGURE 6.4 The ceremonial hall with extended eave and lattice work which screen the sky to reduce glare in the eyes of the visitor

looking up, one sees the roof of the hall, which completely screens the sky. This relationship is carefully designed so that the visitor does not suffer glare from the sky; rather, the eye takes in the beauty of the main pavilion and its forecourt.

The main ceremonial hall is reached up three steps to a platform under a magnificent roof of dark beams and tiles. This is where the family would have received and entertained their guests, in a space diffusely lit via transparent sea-shell-covered screens that fill both the longer sides of the space.

Gable walls are rendered brick incorporating columns to support the roof trusses. The central screen wall opposite the entrance in this hall would normally have been closed, so that members of the family would pass through the doors on either side of the screen to reach the more private domain beyond (Figure 6.5).

One is then within a corridor space. But it is more than a corridor space. Two 'crab eye' light wells bring in reflected light to this space, while also providing the backdrop for a bamboo plant that appears in silhouette like a traditional ink painting, delighting the eye and softening the space. The geometry of these light wells prevents direct sunlight penetration, while bouncing light off the white rendered masonry wall. This diffuse light would have had a psychological as well as physical effect in achieving 'light without heat', compared with the harsh bright light of the outside world (Figure 6.6).

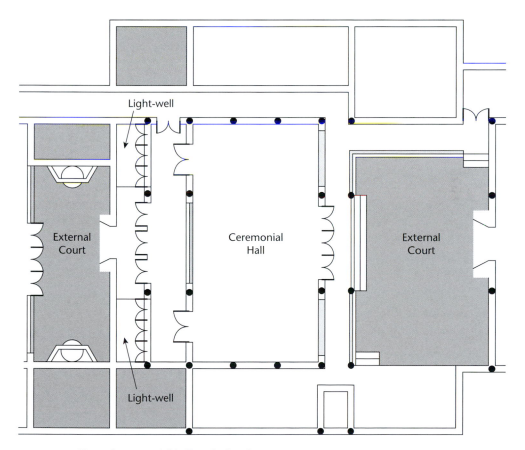

FIGURE 6.5 Plan of ceremonial hall and related courts

FIGURE 6.6 'Crab eye' light – well to the left of ceremonial hall

Entering the first private court, the axis slightly changes and one faces another (smaller) hall, which would have been a family room, with stairs via an adjacent space leading up to bedrooms at first-floor level. This pavilion has similar screens in the walls facing west, and an opaque masonry wall facing east, like the main ceremonial hall, but this time without the 'crab eye' light wells.

A further two narrow courts and single-storey pavilions lead to the back of the house and another narrow canal. Adjacent to the last pavilion, and on the other side of the long service corridor that runs the full length of the house, is a kitchen and tea room, overlooking the narrow canal (Figure 6.7). The land on the other side of this narrow canal has been used to provide a private study (consisting of two pavilions that both address a very private and quiet court) (Figure 6.8), a garden of rocks and cherry trees, and the family temple or shrine (turned to align with the obligatory north/south axis).

Natural cooling through 'crab eye' light wells

In addition to bringing in the reflected light, closer observation reveals a further function for the 'crab eye' light wells. The openable screens that rise from about 500mm from the floor to the ceiling would have been opened in the summer to promote air movement. The screens sit above a low bench, the 'beauty seat' (Figure 6.9), where the ladies of the house apparently sat in the summer. Why did they sit here in this 'corridor'? The answer involves one of the most subtle aspects of this design.

Air from the front of the hall (which has a very large open area) passes through the doors (a much smaller area) and accelerates as it moves across the bench seat and up the 'crab eye'

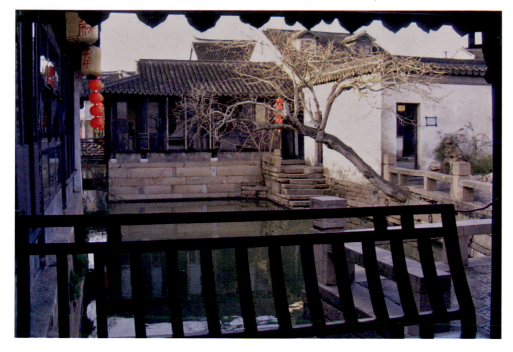

FIGURE 6.7 The canal at the back of Zhang's house

FIGURE 6.8 The private study with the court in front

FIGURE 6.9 'Crab eye' light – well with the beauty seat in front

light wells (spot measurements on a recent visit revealed air velocities of 0.1 to 0.3m/s through the screens at the front of the Hall compared with 0.7 to 1.2m/s through the doors adjacent to the 'beauty seats') (Figure 6.10).

On a hot and humid summer day, this would therefore have been an ideal place to sit: a calm and tranquil place, promoting not just thermal comfort but an experience that combines gentle air movement, the rustle of bamboo leaves, diffuse light from above and oblique views through the hall and into the reception courtyard from where guests would approach.

One can imagine the pleasure and excitement of the ladies of the house on formal occasions, when the house would have provided an exquisite setting for ceremony and entertainment.

The masonry wall to the 'crab eye' light wells provides a second layer of security, as well as protection from the cold easterly and north-easterly winter winds, and acoustic buffer between the public areas and the private rooms of the house behind. This wall also acts like a blank canvas to receive and reveal the beautiful plants in the light wells (Figure 6.11).

Visual delight and comfort

In the eastern part of China, the intense heat and glare from the sun, especially in the summer months, can easily cause overheating and discomfort glare if the building envelope

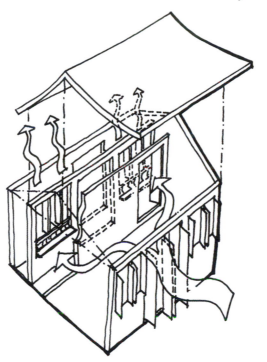

FIGURE 6.10 Axonometric view showing air movement through the hall to 'crab eye' light wells

FIGURE 6.11 'Crab eye' light wells act as wind barrier, picture wall and ventilator

is not designed properly. Colonnades, roof overhangs, lattice work screens and trees had been carefully designed and planted in Zhang's house to reduce the adverse impacts from the sun and glare.

Since Zhang's house has its main entrance facing west, the west-facing façades in the pavilions will be vulnerable to low angle sun in the afternoon. By plotting the sun angles at 3pm on the building section, one can see that the summer sun is blocked out by the colonnades and roof overhangs, while the spring and winter sun can penetrate into the halls and pavilions to warm the interior spaces (Figure 6.12). The glare associated with the low-angle sun is dealt with by the lattice screen windows, doors and trees (Figure 6.13).

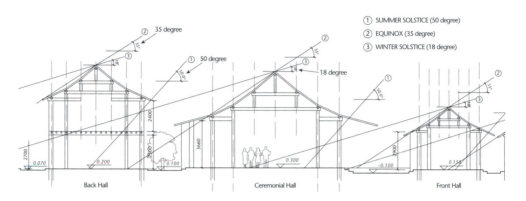

FIGURE 6.12 Section showing the sun angles at 3pm on summer solstice, equinox and winter solstice

FIGURE 6.13 Low-angle winter sun penetrates into the pavilions while the roof overhangs, lattice screen windows and trees reduce glare

In order to reduce the abrupt change of light level between the courts and the pavilions, colonnades and thick stone architraves were used as light 'shields' to reduce the brightness contrast between inside and outside (Figure 6.14).

Spot measurements taken on site under an overcast sky in winter indicate that there is a relatively gentle light fluctuation along the central axis of Zhang's house. The light distribution graph shows that the transitional spaces between the pavilions and the courts, either in the form of colonnades or thick stone architraves, provide adaptation zones for the eyes to adjust to the change of light intensity when one walks though the house (Figure 6.15).

The well-tempered luminous environment here is achieved by the light buffers, the use of colonnades, roof overhangs and lattice windows and thick architraves, which collectively

FIGURE 6.14 Colonnades and thick stone architraves as light shields to reduce brightness contrast

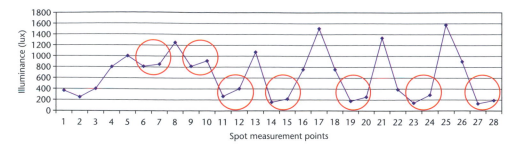

FIGURE 6.15 Zhang's house: light distribution graph with light shields highlighted in circles

reduce excessive brightness contrast and enhance visual perception. The carefully planted trees also act as natural sun screens that are responsive to seasonal changes and further enhance visual comfort and delight.

Conclusion

The multiple functions and the subtle interactions of the different elements attract admiration for the designers of this house. But this is not the work of a single designer (and certainly not a single period). The unique architectural form, space and feature of this house are representative of the traditional houses found in many parts of China, which have developed over millennia.

It is interesting to speculate about the process of the collective and gradual empirically based improvements to achieve such a sublime synthesis. However, the purpose of this study is not to trace this pedigree, but rather to explore how the numerous and subtle ways in which visual and thermal comfort and delight are achieved.

This study is the start of this process. On-site monitoring of light, heat and air is ongoing, to establish whether our claims that such a house really would have been comfortable without air conditioning are valid. Whether this is the case or not, this exquisite house was certainly designed to delight all the senses, and is exemplary in the way that it moderates the impact of the external climate on the well-tempered internal environment.

Acknowledgement

The authors gratefully acknowledge the assistance of the Township Government of Zhouzhuang, and of the Shanghai Research Institute of Building Science.

References

Chen Yi, Zhuang Chundi, Zhang Jihan and Liu Ji (2000) *Nine hundred years old town of Zhouzhuang*, Xi'an, China, Xi'an Map Press.

7

COURTYARDS AND TRANSITIONAL SPACES IN TURKISH TRADITIONAL ARCHITECTURE

Saadet Armağan Güleç, Fatih Canan and Mustafa Korumaz

Introduction

Appropriate solutions that are sensitive to the climate, materials, construction techniques and spatial organization can be observed in the hot–dry climatic regions of south–eastern Turkey. At the urban scale, settlements were sited according to wind patterns and designed to provide shaded spaces in streets. At the building scale, compact forms that helped retain heat gave protection from cold winter months, whereas open space configurations provided shaded spaces for the summer months. The main living units designed for use in the summer months are the *courtyards*, the *eyvan* (covered hall between rooms opening to a courtyard) and the *revak* (porch). This study looks at examples from three cities in south-east Turkey (Figure 7.1), focusing on the most significant spatial organizations of these architectural elements. The authors have also compared the features of these elements with those found on contemporary dwellings in Turkey.

Climate characteristics and urban settlements in south-east Turkey

In south-east Turkey the winter is cold and the summer is generally very hot. In the coldest month (January) the average temperature is 3.7°C rising to 29.8°C in July. The annual average temperature is 16.4°C. The relative humidity is low in this region, evaporation is high in summer and droughts last long owing to rare rainfall. For a hot-dry climate the most appropriate site for a

MAP 7 Diyarbakır, Turkey

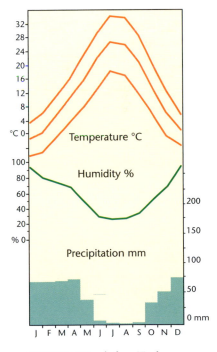

GRAPH 7 Diyarbakır, Turkey

FIGURE 7.1 Location of the three cities from south-east Turkey: Diyarbakır, Urfa and Mardin

settlement is a valley floor where cooler weather usually prevails. Because valley floors are flatter than hills, summer warming-up is less, making them better suited for comfort (Akşit, 2006). Of the three cities discussed here, Urfa and its surrounding urban settlements are located on a large plain. For this reason, the streets are wider. Mardin occupies a hilly terrain terraced towards the prevailing wind. Its streets up the hill are narrow and for pedestrians only. Diyarbakır is a city bordered by a defensive wall and was designed accordingly as a dense urban settlement. Its small footprint also explains the compact nature of its houses (Nurtekin, 1999). Privacy considerations determined the orientation of the houses. Because of narrow streets few windows and other openings faced to the street or the neighbouring yard. Living spaces were arranged around courtyards of roughly square form.

Traditional architectural solutions

Courtyard

The courtyard is the most significant feature of buildings in this region. It is an open space surrounded by living spaces. The usage of individual courtyards varied according to lifestyles, habits, customs and social and economic standing of the inhabitants. Gardens, landscape elements and water ponds enriched the courtyard visually as well as improving its microclimate (Erdoğan, 1996). Courtyards situated at the entrances of some houses were of varying sizes depending on the size of the house plot. In Urfa the courtyards are square or rectangular in form. Entering through the garden door, one reached the courtyard from a narrow corridor, the *kapı arası*. On the house walls surrounding the courtyard, there are unglazed openings located high up used to take away fumes and odours from indoor spaces.

The main rooms of Urfa houses are oriented to the north, and their floor levels are 1.5–2.0m above the floor level of the courtyard, while other rooms are some 0.50m above the courtyard (Figures 7.2 and 7.3) (Şenocak, 1990). The longest side of rooms was usually along the courtyard with windows on this side. These rooms were ventilated by small rectangular or round windows known in the region as *ışık takası*. These small openings were also effective for ventilation in the cold season, so that the larger windows would not need to be opened in cold weather. In the historical houses of Urfa, water generally features at the centre of the courtyard in the form of a well or a water trough known as *cürun* in Turkish (Özdem, 2002). In some other houses the well was located in the kitchen, which opened directly on to the courtyard (Şenocak, 1990).

In Mardin the courtyards are large terraces opening towards the valley. High walls ensure intimacy and safety (Figures 7.4 and 7.5). The larger houses of Mardin featured several courtyards that were located at different levels. The city's dense dwelling fabric prevented the development of gardens, and vegetation did not have an important role in the spatial organization of the courtyard. Where used, the principal trees for the courtyard were mulberry trees, plum trees and grapevines.

In the dense urban fabric of Diyarbakır, the courtyards were the only parts of the house that had some connection with nature (Figures 7.6 and 7.7). Despite an often deformed geometry the courtyard remains close to a rectangular form. If the street layout obliges a deformation of the courtyard's geometry, one edge of the rectangle follows the layout of the street (Tuncer, 1999). It reaches the courtyard through a narrow passage known as *sokak arası* in Turkish. All parts of the house are generally directed towards the courtyard.

Orientation influenced the shape of the house and led to the creation of specific spaces for seasonal activities. The rest area for the summer is always placed to the south of the courtyard. The winter areas are generally to the north of the courtyard, which allows them to have a southern orientation. Alternatively, winter spaces are positioned to the east. The spring areas may be located to the east or west of the courtyard (Özdem, 2002). These are encountered in houses of rich families only. The winter and summer areas can be seen in all the traditional houses of Diyarbakır. The water ponds of the courtyard are always at the centre of the *eyvan*. The most important passive cooling systems of Diyarbakır houses are the *serdap*. These are spaces located at basement level that are kept cool by contact with the ground and the flow of water on its way to the water pond. These spaces have been known in this area for a long time as *selsal*, a kind of fountain (Sözen, 1971). In the traditional houses of Diyarbakır the garden is the focus of the courtyard, with grapevine and mulberry trees in almost every house.

Eyvan

The *eyvan* is a semi-open transitional space located between a courtyard and a dwelling's inhabitable rooms (Figure 7.8). It is a covered space enclosed within the building plan on three sides and opening to the courtyard on the fourth (Figure 7.9). The *eyvan* acts as a common semi-outdoor living area between a pair of rooms. Its relation to the outside open areas is very important (Gençosmanoğlu and Özdemir, 2005). It should be a shaded, cool rest space for the summer. The *eyvan* orientation towards the south or east is appropriate for this climate for protection against the mid-afternoon sun. The *eyvan* is also generally provided with a window on its north wall. This window ensures cross-ventilation to keep the space cool.

FIGURE 7.2 Plan and view of courtyard of Hacı Hafızlar House, Urfa

Source: Şenocak, 1990

FIGURE 7.3 Plan and view of courtyard of Hacı Tevfik Saraç House, Urfa

Source: Şenocak, 1990

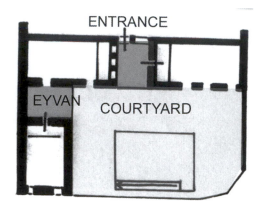

FIGURE 7.4 Plan and view of the house at 113 street no: 18, Mardin

Source: Alioğlu, 2000

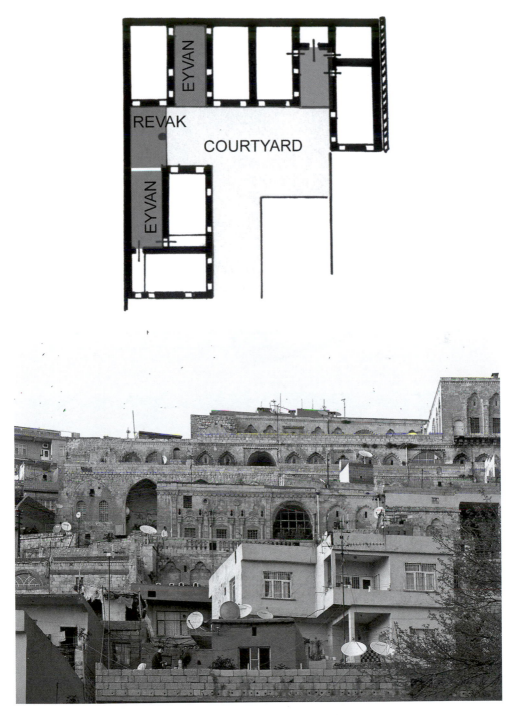

FIGURE 7.5 Plan and view of the house at 110 street no: 8, Mardin

Source: Alioğlu, 2000

FIGURE 7.6 Plan and view of house on 197 parcel 11, Diyarbakır

Source: Tuncer, 1999

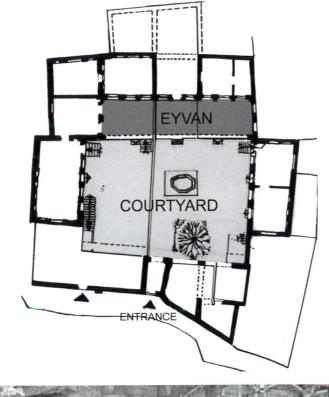

FIGURE 7.7 Plan and view of house on 190 parcel 1, Diyarbakır

Source: Tuncer, 1999

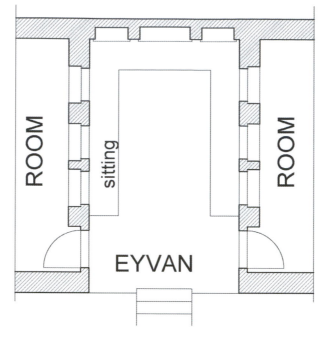

FIGURE 7.8 Plan of *eyvan*

FIGURE 7.9 View of *eyvan* from the courtyard

In the region discussed in this study, the *eyvan* is of the same degree of importance as the courtyard. In traditional Urfa houses, the north wall of the *eyvan* incorporates a chimney that contributes to airflow (Figure 7.10) (Şenocak 1990). A water pond was sometimes placed in the *eyvan* to reinforce the cooling effect. Access to the courtyard was down a set of steps off a narrow balcony about 1.0m wide know as a *gezenek* and supported by stone columns on the courtyard (Figure 7.11). Under the *eyvan* were the cellars, earth-coupled cooler spaces in which food was preserved. Similar configurations of the *eyvan* are found in the traditional houses of Mardin (Seyhan, 1999) and on those of Diyarbakır (Sözen, 1971) where the *eyvan* are often the largest spaces of the house.

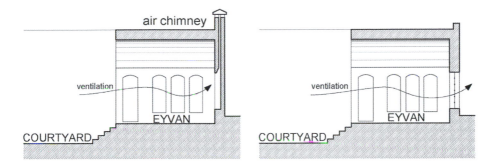

FIGURE 7.10 Section of *evyan* showing variants

FIGURE 7.11 Gezenek balcony in Urfa

Revak

The *revak* has features that are common to all three cities. It is a shaded, semi-open space along the courtyard and also a place where the animals were attached (Figure 7.2) (Alioğlu, 2000). Compared to the *eyvan*, the *revak* has a more open frontage.

Kabaltı

Rooms built above an arch bridging a street provided extra space while creating a cooler, shaded space at street level below (Figure 7.12). This became a play area for children and place of rest for older people. In Urfa, where the summer period lasts more than six months, there are several examples of these vaulted structures. The street surface was covered in basalt stone and the cover over the street extended to some 5–10 metres.

Open and semi-open spaces in contemporary housing

Balconies and terraces have replaced the courtyard, the *eyvan* and the *revak* on current housing. They have various sizes and forms (Figure 7.13). On detached houses terraces are situated between living spaces and the garden. They are mostly smaller than the traditional courtyards. The size varies from house to house and may be limited by building and planning codes. Balconies are a common element of apartment buildings. They are mostly smaller than terraces with a depth commonly limited to 1.5m (Figures 7.14 to 7.16).

Although contemporary dwellings have semi-outdoor spaces and landscape elements in their gardens, these are not specially designed as courtyards were in the past. Their integration with the building is not as strong, and their microclimatic effects are not as effective. Water elements, which provided moisture and evaporative cooling effect in courtyards, are much reduced today.

The importance that was given to these elements in traditional architecture is also reflected in the proportion of dwellings' floor area that they occupied. An estimate of this based on the houses illustrated in Figures 7.2–7.7 is shown in Figure 7.17. These are based on the ground floor areas of the dwellings. A comparison can be drawn with contemporary housing based on the most common apartment typologies built today. This shows that on the traditional houses the areas of open and semi-open spaces add up to 40–45 per cent of the dwellings' floor area, whereas in current housing the percentage of total floor area represented by terraces is only 20–25 per cent (Figure 7.17).

Conclusions

The study of the open spaces of traditional houses of Urfa, Mardin and Diyarbakır provided important lessons on the environmental role of these spaces, and on features that are missing from today's buildings, which we must adapt from traditional architecture.

FIGURE 7.12
Kabaltı rooms, Urfa

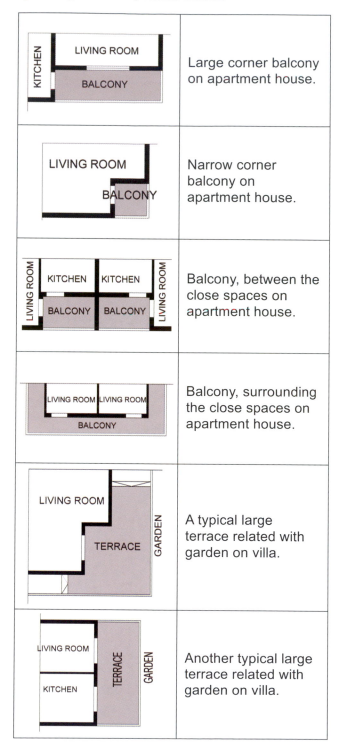

LIVING ROOM / KITCHEN / BALCONY	Large corner balcony on apartment house.
LIVING ROOM / BALCONY	Narrow corner balcony on apartment house.
LIVING ROOM / KITCHEN / KITCHEN / LIVING ROOM / BALCONY / BALCONY	Balcony, between the close spaces on apartment house.
LIVING ROOM / LIVING ROOM / BALCONY	Balcony, surrounding the close spaces on apartment house.
LIVING ROOM / TERRACE / GARDEN	A typical large terrace related with garden on villa.
LIVING ROOM / KITCHEN / TERRACE / GARDEN	Another typical large terrace related with garden on villa.

FIGURE 7.13 General typologies of open and semi-open spaces in current houses

FIGURE 7.14 Widespread balcony examples on apartments in this region

FIGURE 7.15 Widespread terrace and balcony examples on villas in this region

FIGURE 7.16 Current urban tissue without consideration of orientation and climate

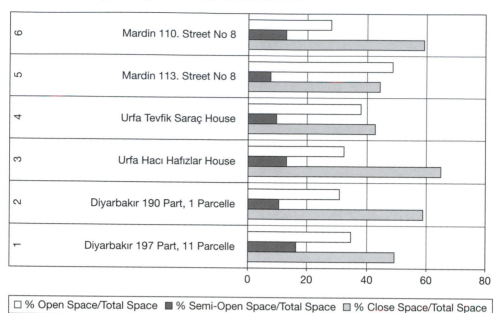

FIGURE 7.17 Open and semi–open spaces as percent of total ground floor area of traditional
buildings

References

Akşit, J. F. (2006) 'Türkiye'nin Farklı İklim Bölgelerinde Enerji Etkin Bina ve Yerleşme Birimi Tasarımı',
Tasarım, İstanbul, vol. 157, p.125.

Alioğlu, E. F. (2000) 'Mardin Şehir Dokusu ve Evler', Istanbul, Türkiye Ekonomik ve Toplumsal Tarih
Vakfı Yayını (A publication of the Turkish Economic and Social History Foundation), pp.69, 81–83.

Erdoğan, E. (1996) 'Anadolu Avlularının Özellik ve Düzenleme İlkeleri', PhD Thesis, Ankara University,
Ankara, p.35.

Gençosmanoğlu, A. B. and Özdemir, İ. M. (2005) 'Metamorphism in culture and housing design: Turkey
as an example', *Building and Environment*, p.1446. (Paper also available on www.elsevier.com.)

Nurtekin Ö. (1999) 'Diyarbakır Suriçi Evlerinin Ekolojik Yönden İncelenmesi', Masters Thesis, Ankara.

Özdem, F. (2002) 'Uygarlıklar kapısı Urfa', Istanbul, Yapı Kredi Publications.

Seyhan, E. (1999) 'Mardin Evlerinde Mekan Kurgusu', Master's Thesis, Istanbul, p.82.

Şenocak, İ M. (1990) 'Şanlıurfa'da Geleneksel Mimarimiz', MSc Thesis, Selcuk University, Konya, pp.91,
93, 96.

Sözen, M. (1971) 'Diyarbakır'da Türk Mimarisi', p.51, Istanbul, Diyarbakırı Tanıtma ve Turizm
Derneği Yayınları (A publication of the Diyarbakır Tourist Association).

Tuncer, O. C. (1999) 'Diyarbakır Evleri', Diyarbakır, Department of Cultural and Art of Diyarbakır
Metropolitan Municipality, pp.39, 314–330.

PART II
Vernacular Architecture as Model

8

APPLYING THE LESSONS OF INDIAN VERNACULAR ARCHITECTURE

The bungalow

Kimberly Kramer

MAP 8 Bengali Baharampur, India

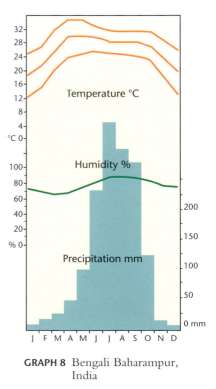

GRAPH 8 Bengali Baharampur, India

Introduction

Britain's official involvement in India began as a purely mercantile concern, with the founding of the East India Company in 1600 to challenge the century-long Portuguese monopoly of the spice trade. France, Sweden, Denmark and the Netherlands also entered the Asian spice market around this time, each establishing trading posts in India. Until the middle of the eighteenth century, the extent of European control was limited to small trading settlements along the coasts, but a series of battles between 1757 and 1764 expanded the area of European control considerably and marked the beginning of Britain's political, commercial and military hegemony in India. By 1818, the British conquest of India was effectively complete, and the interior of India, previously largely closed to Europeans, was opened to the military and administrative armies of the British Empire.

The political shift in the mid-eighteenth century created a shift in British settlement patterns as well. As their settlements grew and spread into the interior, British settlers were faced with the challenge of building comfortable and affordable dwellings in a climate very different from their own. Taking many of their cues from traditional local architecture, the settlers developed a new building form. Commonly known as the *bungalow*, it incorporated and adapted many traditional Indian strategies for improving climatic response to create a dwelling built to meet European expectations of both form and comfort.

Origins

Early British settlement in India

The first British citizens in India were merchants rather than settlers. Until the mid-eighteenth century, most Britons spent a brief career in India living in the East India Company's fortified 'factories' on the edges of the country. These factories were in an urban setting, either inside newly constructed forts, for security purposes, or in converted native buildings (Figure 8.1). They were fortified compounds containing accommodations, offices and storehouses, which have been described as 'the commercial counterpart of a University college', where 'even the chiefs were rarely accompanied by their wives, and the others were not expected to marry . . . Meals were taken in common . . . there were daily prayers, and the gates were closed at stated hours' (Roberts, 1952).

The other main British presence in India before the mid-eighteenth century was the military, which had a similar settlement pattern of small defensible compounds and communal life. Like their merchant counterparts, the soldiers adopted ready-made shelter when possible, generally in the form of canvas service tents carried from Britain (Figure 8.2). When they did build, they built primarily for security.

FIGURE 8.1 Factory of the East India Company, seventeenth century

Source: King, 1984

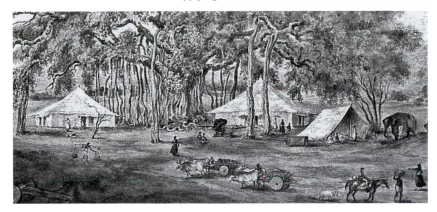

FIGURE 8.2 British army service tents in India

Source: King, 1984

After the military victories in the middle of the eighteenth century, the British in India began to look beyond the goal of commercial exploitation to the possibility of settlement and control (Harrison, 1999, p.59). As British power in India continued to grow, settlers began to emerge from the relative safety of the factory and military camp to settle the interior of the country.

This expansion created a need for a new building pattern. Neither the factory nor the military camp provided a suitable model for independent settlement at such a large scale. Designed for security and intended only for temporary housing, they also made few concessions to environmental comfort in the harsh Indian climate. The new settlers would have to look elsewhere for an appropriate housing model as they began to settle the interior of India.

Climatic conditions

The first large expansion of British settlement in the mid-eighteenth century was centred in Bengal, an area on the east coast of India, stretching to the north and west of Calcutta. As they moved from the relative comfort of the coast into the interior of Bengal, the British settlers encountered a climate very different from their own. One Englishman who experienced the difference first-hand in the early 1800s wrote, 'Were I disposed to pursue a contrast betwixt the climate of Bengal and that of England; it would be easy to turn the scale on either side' (Ward, 1818/1999).

While the English climate is temperate, that of Bengal is tropical. The plains that make up most of the southern region are hot and humid all year except for the short winter season. The temperature in the hills and mountains in the north is cooler, but the humidity is still high. The hot season lasts from March to early June, with daytime temperatures ranging from 38 to 45°C across the region. The monsoon arrives in mid-June and lasts through September. Autumn is mild, and lasts until mid-November, when winter sets in. Winter on the plains is also mild, with minimum temperatures rarely dropping below 15°C. Rainfall is rare in winter, averaging only 0.1 inches (2.54mm) in December compared to 13 inches (330mm) in August. The humidity is thus substantially reduced, making winter a very pleasant season on the plains. The cold season lasts for about three months, and is followed by a brief month-long mild spring season. Summer heat arrives again in mid-March (*Encyclopaedia Britannica*, 2001*).*

Vernacular influences

The architectural and climatic adaptations that the British had developed for their own temperate climate were not applicable in this new environment. The traditional English country house or cottage model was inappropriate in a number of ways. An English house was generally built as a tightly closed box to minimize drafts wherever possible. This was sensible in a cold climate, but not appropriate in a hot, humid climate where a bit of breeze is quite valuable in enhancing the cooling effect of evaporation. The traditional band of large south-facing windows which, in England, allowed valuable warmth from the sun to gather in the cooler months, would also have been wholly inappropriate in the hot and relentlessly sunny Indian climate where the sun's penetration must be tightly controlled.

The earliest British settlers in India, concerned with trade and security rather than long-term settlement, had not developed an environmentally appropriate building model for the Indian climate. Even the canvas service tents of the military, though similar in form to the simple thatched huts of the local population, were not wholly appropriate. Without the shading of a thick thatch roof, the inside temperature rose quickly. The memoirs of one traveller who went to India in 1765 record that 'in the soldiers' tents, composed only of a single canvas, Farenheit's [*sic*] thermometer often rose to 116 degrees [47°C]. . . This exceeded every thing I had before experienced, and had it continued long no European constitution could have supported it' (James, 1813/1999).

As the British settlers moved out of the factories and military camps to settle the interior of the country, they sought a form of affordable and reasonably comfortable dwelling that could be built with the abundant local labour. The factory model was no longer appropriate, and because the settlers were dependent on local labour outside of the cities, much of the form was adopted from the local vernacular tradition.

The traditional Bengali dwelling provided a model for the British bungalow designs that developed. Travellers' accounts provide a fairly consistent account of these buildings, which are generally referred to as *bangla* (or *banggolo*). The *bangla* was a thatched hut, generally built with a distinctively curved roof. The walls were generally made of mud. Where the mud was not suitable for this purpose, walls were constructed of bunches of straw or mats, tied to each other and to the bamboo frame to form walls. Where straw was used, it was often plastered with cow dung and clay (Buchanan, 1810/1984, p.19).

The frame of a *bangla* was typically constructed entirely of bamboo, though wood posts and beams were occasionally used in the houses of the very wealthy. The thatched roof generally extended beyond the walls to provide additional shelter from the rains, and one side of the roof was often extended four or five feet beyond the wall and supported by a row of bamboo poles to create a small veranda, sometimes used as a shop. Contemporary accounts and images give no indication of a consistent orientation for this veranda.

In many *banglas,* the door was the only opening, 'crevices excepted' (Buchanan, 1810/1984, p.19). In the houses of the very wealthy, this opening might be covered by a wooden door that folded from the side. In most cases, however, it was shut by a hurdle (*jhangp*) which was tied to the upper part of the door and either propped open or left down to shut the door

FIGURE 8.3 Peasant dwelling, Bengal: the window of this dwelling is shaded by a *jhangp*, which has been propped open.

Source: King, 1984

(King, 1984, p.21). Windows, when present, were shaded in the same way (Figure 8.3). Floors were made of mud and were generally raised a foot or two above the ground to provide some protection from flooding (Williamson, 1810/1984, p.31).

In describing these native dwellings, Francis Buchanan, a European traveller, wrote in 1810:

> The style of private edifice that is proper and peculiar to Bengal, consists of a hut with a pent roof constructed of two sloping sides which meet in a ridge forming the segment of a circle so that it has a resemblance to a boat when overturned . . . This kind of hut, it is said, from being peculiar to Bengal, is called by the native Banggolo . . . Where the materials admit, the walls of the hut are made of mud and the floor is always raised a foot or two above the level of the plain, but not always so high as to be above water in the rainy season; so that a platform of bamboos is then constructed at one end of the hut and upon this the family sit and sleep while they must wade through the mud to reach the door.
>
> (Buchanan, 1810/1984, pp.18–19)

Buchanan's account is supported by contemporary drawings by George Chinnery and by later photographs, which show both the distinctive roof shape and the gallery extending to one side (Figures 8.4 and 8.5).

The size of the huts varied little. Most were between 4×3m and 4×5m (King, 1984, pp.18, 20). 'Among the natives', notes Buchanan, 'the poor man has one hut for himself and cattle, the richer men increase the number without altering the plan of the building' (King, 1984, pp.18, 20). While a 'common labourer' might have only one hut for himself and his family,

FIGURE 8.4 Peasant dwelling, Bengal, George Chinnery, 1813

Source: King, 1984

FIGURE 8.5 Rural Bengal, photograph by Samuel Bourne, 1860s

Source: King, 1984

a wealthy family might have as many as ten, used for different purposes. Anthony King, in his study of the bungalow form, notes that:

> In other regions of India, single households are frequently accommodated in single dwellings, separated into rooms or spaces . . . Whether the multiplication of the single, simple hut in the Bengal peasant household resulted from structural limitations of bamboo building materials or other cultural factors is not clear.
>
> (King, 1984, pp.18, 20)

Another possible explanation for this peculiarity may be climatic adaptation, as in the humid region of Bengal, small buildings scattered to allow air movement between them could help to maximize the effects of any available breeze (Olgyay, 1963, p.5).

There appear to have been three main variations in the shape of the thatched roof among the native huts, leading some historians to divide them into three different types of structures. The most common was the distinctively curved roof, often illustrated in travellers' accounts and drawings. There does not seem to have been a significant climatic advantage to this shape (conversation with Nick Baker, 22 November 2005), though the lack of ridges at the joints of each slope, may have made it slightly less vulnerable to leaking in the rainy season (Cooper, 1998, p. 169). In some dwellings, the roof had a simpler shape, with four sloped faces joining at the apex to form a pyramid. Where the sides were not of even length, the longer sides of the roof would join to form a ridge line. The third form was similar to the second, but the roof was divided into two sections with a clerestory between for light and ventilation (Figure 8.6). This last form represents a clear advantage in a hot humid climate, where breeze is at a premium and indirect daylighting is ideal. However, it seems to have been common only among the rich.

Form and climatic response

The traditional Bengali hut, and the climatic adaptations that it embodied, provided the model for the British bungalow, the main housing form in the expansion of the British settlements. The main characteristics of the European bungalow in India were the pitched thatched roof, the veranda, the raised base platform, and the free-standing single-storey structure (Figure 8.7). The British also seem to have adopted the custom of keeping multiple small buildings rather than one large one. The general adoption of these features is confirmed by contemporary accounts. Two particularly useful accounts are those written by two Englishmen at the end of the eighteenth and the beginning of the nineteenth century, when the English bungalow came into being as a distinct architectural form. In these accounts, the Englishmen struggle to relate the form to something familiar to the home audience, comparing it to both the military service tent and the English cottage.

In 1803, a young army officer, Henry Roberdeau, wrote:

> The Englishmen live in what are really stationary tents which have run aground on low brick platforms. They are 'Bungalows', a word I know not how to render unless by a Cottage. These are always thatched with straw on the roof and the walls are sometimes of bricks and often of mats. Some have glass windows besides the Venetians but this is not very common . . . To hide the sloping roof we put up a kind of artificial

FIGURE 8.6 Pyramidal roofs with clerestory, Vishnapur, West Bengal
Source: Cooper, 1998

FIGURE 8.7 Early form of Englishman's bungalow
Source: Atkinson, 1859/1911

ceiling made of white cloth . . . There are curtains over the doorway to keep out the wind . . . I have two Bungalows near to each other, in one I sleep and dress and in the other, sit and eat.

(Nilsson, 1968, p.187)

The Europeans seem to have adopted almost universally the simple or elongated pyramidal roof, sometimes with clerestory. The ventilation effects of the clerestory may have been impaired somewhat by the white cloth that was generally hung to make what Roberdeau calls an 'artificial ceiling'. Different accounts note different reasons for this innovation, from improving appearance and protecting from dirt and bugs falling from the thatch, to improving the acoustics for musical performances (Williamson, 1810/1984, p.31).

Because of the problems of white ants and warping, as well as the echoing of footsteps where 'menials . . . are ever moving about' (Williamson, 1810/1984, p.31), Europeans eschewed the wood board floors that they were familiar with for the traditional Bengali mud floor, raised on a mud-brick platform to prevent flooding in the monsoon season.

The British settlers expanded the traditional veranda to encircle the house, often semi-enclosing it with permeable mat or brick walls to increase privacy and shade while preserving breezes (Grant, 1849/1984, p.27). To control the sun, the British adopted the Indian use of *jhangps* rolled shades ('tatties') or Venetians to shade both windows and verandas.

The corners of the veranda were often partitioned off as separate rooms for bathing or sleeping, thus providing for British notions of privacy while preserving air flow around and through each room (Figure 8.8). This basic form later developed and became more complex, though the size and complexity of the floor plan was limited by the necessity of maintaining airflow around and through each room (Figure 8.9). Even large estates were

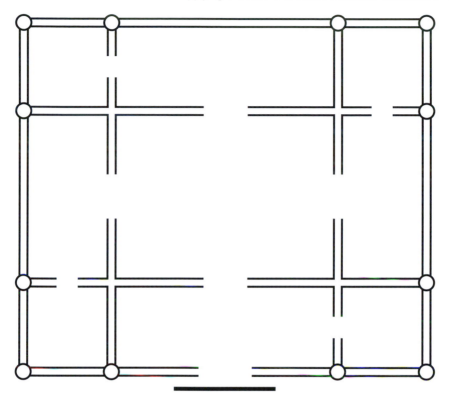

FIGURE 8.8 Bungalow plan with partitioned corners

Source: King, 1984

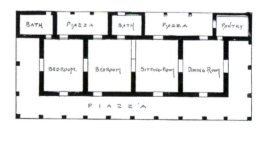

FIGURE 8.9 Developed bungalow forms: each room opens onto a veranda (also referred to as a piazza) on at least two sides to take advantage of the cooled air and to allow access to any available breeze

Source: Kipling, 1911

generally composed of a moderately sized great house and a number of smaller bungalows used to accommodate guests and for other household functions.

Limitations

Despite the advantages of climatically appropriate dwellings, British settlers continued to struggle to adapt to the tropical climate of Bengal. This was, in large part, due to a general reluctance to change their behaviour to suit the demands of the climate. English settlers and military men continued to take large, heavy lunches and to walk out in the noon sun, when the locals stayed inside. One naval surgeon lamented that Europeans often injured themselves in India:

> from a kind of false bravado, and the exhibition of a generous contempt for what they reckon the luxurious and effeminate practices of the country . . . Perhaps they will not even carry an umbrella to screen them from the rays of the sun, but will ramble about, and take their former exercise in the heat of the day, till some climate sickness is brought on, and teaches them . . . to distinguish between what the inhabitants of the country have learned from experience . . . and their own erroneous and rash conjectures (Harrison, 1999, p.87).

To encourage more rational behaviour, Company servant James Forbes composed a short poem to prepare the youth of England for their encounter with the East. The last two stanzas read:

> Observe the Hindoo, whose untutor'd mind,
> All false seductive luxury declines;
> To Nature's wants his wishes are confined,
> While Health her empire o'er his frame maintains.
> His modes of life, by ancient sages plann'd,
> To suit the temper of his burning skies,
> He, who the climate's rage would long withstand,
> Will wisely imitate, nor e'er despise!

> (Forbes, 1999, p. 86)

The British also forced upon themselves the disadvantage of inappropriate dress (Figure 8.10). Formal European dress was required of military and civil servants on most public occasions. Though some relaxed their customs with time, the increasing number of British citizens in India and the resultant formalization of British life there through the end of the eighteenth and into the nineteenth century only reinforced the problem. In 1836, James Johnson, in his treatise *Economy of Health*, commented on the continuing problem of climatically inappropriate dress:

> The necessity which tyrant custom – perhaps policy, has imposed upon us, of continuing to appear in European dress – particularly *uniform*, on almost all public occasions . . . under a burning sky, is not one of the least miseries of a tropical life! It is true, that this ceremony is often waved, in the more social circles that gather round the supper-table, where the light, cool, and elegant vesture of the East supersedes the cumbrous

garb of northern climates. It is certainly laughable, or rather pitiable enough, to behold, for some time after each fresh importation from Europe, a number of *griffinish* sticklers for decorum, whom no persons can induce to cast their *exuvioe*, even in the most affable company, pinioned, as it were, in their stiff habiliments, while the streams of perspiration that issue from every pore, and ooze through various angles of their dress, might almost incline us to fear that they were on the point of realizing Hamlet's wish; and that, in good earnest, their 'Solid flesh would melt − Thaw, and resolve itself into a dew!'

(Johnson, 1836/1999, p.84)

Because their habits of behaviour and expectations of thermal comfort remained largely unchanged when faced with the realities of the Bengali climate, maintaining thermal comfort for the British settlers became a very labour-intensive process, powered by abundant and cheap local labour (Figure 8.11). During hot periods, servants would splash the 'tatties' with water to cool the breezes that passed through them and into the house (King, 1984, p.34). Servants were also utilized to operate *punkahs*, heavy cloths hung from the ceiling and attached to a rope, which a servant pulled to wave the cloth and create a breeze (Figure 8.12).

English households in India typically employed a large domestic staff − in this case, nineteen servants − who were responsible for the labour-intensive process of maintaining thermal comfort.

One cultural importation was well applied in the Indian context. During the hot summer months, when even the *punkah* was insufficient to maintain an acceptable comfort level, the British settlers in Bengal simply left the heat of the plains and took refuge in the relative cool of the hills to the north. Many settlers maintained a second home in the hills (Figure 8.13), and the change of climate was thought to be so beneficial to health that the 'government very liberally built a number of small bungalows in airy situations around it, for the

FIGURE 8.10 The Rev. J. F. Cole's bungalow: a large bungalow with clerestory, shaded veranda, open park and a number of servants. Note the dark, heavy dress of the Reverend's wife, in the left foreground

Source: King, 1984

FIGURE 8.11 Abundant local labour

Source: King, 1984

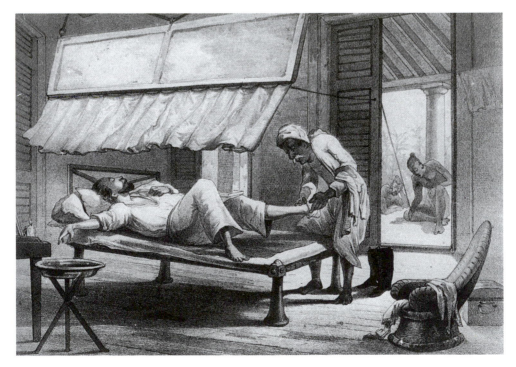

FIGURE 8.12 Labour-intensive thermal control: one servant operates a *punkah* while another
brings a change of clothes

Source: King, 1984

FIGURE 8.13 Bungalow as hill station and second home
Source: King, 1984

accommodation, gratis, of any of their civil or military servants who might come . . . for their health' (Heber, 1828/1984, p.36).

Conclusion

The case of the British settlers in India seems to present an interesting contradiction: in spite of the climatic adaptations adopted from the local vernacular architectural tradition, a well-designed building was able to make up only some of the difference between European expectations of thermal comfort and the realities of the Bengali climate. Still, the British settlers were unwilling to change their daily behavioural patterns to suit the climate as they had their houses. Why would a group of settlers so quick to adopt a new form of dwelling be so reticent to change their patterns of exercise and dress for similar advantages?

The answer may be that the development of the European bungalow as a dwelling form was not a choice but a compromise resulting from circumstances on the ground. The British citizens who settled India were not 'settlers' in the true sense of the word. They were generally merchants, officers and diplomats who simply found themselves in need of a house. Unlike early emigrants in North America, Australia or South Africa, who built their new dwellings with their own hands according to the cultural models in their heads (King, 1984, p. 30), the British citizens who spread across Bengal had access to ready and cheap native labour. Even the common soldier had servants of his own. The British 'settlers' focused on their own civil or military roles in the expanding British government in India, and depended on local labour for the construction of their dwellings. Though they may have had a different form in mind, the execution of the design was in the hands of the native labour force, and the result was often very much a native product. King notes that 'The persistence of Indian "housing models" over those of the European patrons for whom they were built was a frequent source of amusement' (King, 1984, p.30).

While it may not have been their ideal, the European-style bungalow did provide its tenants with a climatically appropriate housing model so effective and affordable that it soon became a standard, reproduced throughout India and eventually imported in a modified form to Britain and America. Its proliferation is a testament to its effectiveness in striking a compromise between the oft-opposing European expectations of form and comfort.

Acknowledgement

Thanks are due to the many scholars whose work I consulted in my research, particularly Anthony King, whose excellent study of the evolving bungalow form is oft cited in this essay.

References

Atkinson, G. F. (1859/1911) 'Curry and rice', London, Day & Son, 1859, in J. L. Kipling, 'The origin of the bungalow', *Country Life in America*, vol. 19, no 8, p.308.

Buchanan, F. (1810/1984) quotation in A. King, *The Bungalow*, London, Routledge & Kegan Paul.

Cooper, I. (1998) *Traditional Buildings of India*, London: Thames and Hudson.

Encyclopaedia Britannica (2001) 'West Bengal: climate', standard edition CD-ROM; also available at: www.webindia123.com/westbengal/land/climate.htm (accessed 7 December 2005).

Forbes, J. (1999) quotation in M. Harrison, *Climates and Constitutions*, New Delhi, Oxford University Press.

Grant, C. (1849/1984) 'Anglo-Indian domestic life', in A. King, *The Bungalow,* London, Routledge & Kegan Paul.

Harrison, M. (1999) *Climates and Constitutions,* New Delhi, Oxford University Press.

Heber, Bishop (1828/1984) quotation in A. King, *The Bungalow*, London, Routledge & Kegan Paul.

James, J. (1813/1999) 'Oriental memoirs: selected from a series of familiar letters written during seventeen years residence in India', in M. Harrison, *Climates and Constitutions*, New Delhi, Oxford University Press, pp.61–62.

Johnson, J. (1836/1999) 'Economy of health', in M. Harrison, *Climates and Constitutions*, New Delhi, Oxford University Press.

King, A. (1984) *The Bungalow*, London: Routledge & Kegan Paul.

Kipling, J. L. (1911) 'The origin of the bungalow', *Country Life in America*, vol. 19, no 8, pp.309–310.

Nilsson, S. (1968) *European Architecture in India 1750–1850*, London: Faber and Faber.

Olgyay, V. (1963) *Design with Climate*, Princeton NJ: Princeton University Press.

Roberts, P. E. (1952) *History of British India*, London, Geoffrey Cumberlege, p.75.

Ward, W. (1818/1999) 'A view of the history, literature, and mythology, of the Hindoos' (1818), in M. Harrison, *Climates and Constitutions*, New Delhi, Oxford University Press, p.58.

Williamson, T. (1810/1984) quotation in A. King, *The Bungalow*, London, Routledge & Kegan Paul.

9

LIGHTING FEATURES IN JAPANESE TRADITIONAL ARCHITECTURE

José María Cabeza-Lainez

Introduction

It has often been said that Japan is a land of contrasts. This is clearly seen when we consider the extreme variety of its climates. Tall mountains perpetually powdered with snow coexist with places that experience scorching summer heat, and the dryness of the winter is followed by an extreme degree of humidity in monsoon-marked weather. As with many other regions of the world, Japanese architecture has evolved through the years in accordance with climatic factors. However, there is an important distinction in that in Japan reverence for the environment is the main feature of sacred architecture and thus it is found here more steadily than in civil or even vernacular buildings. There is a general belief supported by Shintô religion that the land belongs to natural spirits (the *kami*) and permission to dwell in a place should be obtained by the builders. The way to receive this boon is to follow the architectural traditions and to observe ceremonies such as the *tatemae* (literally: before con-struction). An example that demonstrates the importance of sunlight for the Japanese is a report from age old chronicles mentioning that Amaterasu the Sun goddess, during a period of seclusion from worldly affairs, deprived the land of light. Upon her return, She bestowed on her sibling, the first emperor Ninigi, a holy mirror spelling the words: 'Thou shalt worship this Mirror as if it wert My August Spirit' (*Kojiki*, 1992). The mirror is treasured today at Ise Shrine as pledge of the alliance between humans and heaven.

MAP 9 Kyoto, Japan

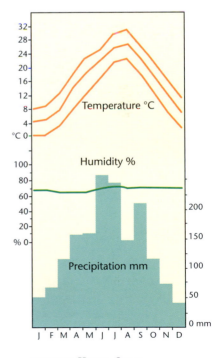

GRAPH 9 Kyoto, Japan

Vernacular examples

In accordance with the above, traditional architecture, whether sacred or popular, has always devised smart features to deal with light and the sun (Figure 9.1). One of these features is the *shôji*, a tiny wooden lattice, covered with sheets of oiled paper that are relatively impervious and resistant to the wind, that works as a kind of sliding door and window (Figure 9.2). The *shôji* is not transparent, but we have measured that it has a solar transmittance of 0.5–0.6 depending on time and weather conditions. It thus helps prevent being overlooked, but provides only limited protection from the direct sun. On the other hand, when the sky is cloudy the *shôji* produces pleasant though gloomy interiors. These interiors seem to be appreciated by the Japanese people and are the subject of a celebrated essay *In praise of shadows* by the novelist Junichiro Tanizaki (Tanizaki, 1977).

We have performed a lighting simulation for a model of a typical house in Kôbe, assuming that the main walls are made of *shôji* and taking into account the likely influence of the eaves (*noki*). The procedure followed by the simulation is based on radiative transfer of flux as described by Cabeza-Lainez (2006). The simulation was performed for 1200 hours solar time (noon) under overcast sky and for clear sky with sun between June and December near the solstices (Figures 9.3 and 9.4).

At certain times of the day, if the room becomes too dark, the only solution is to slide the *shôji* open to increase the admission of daylight. However, this may expose the room to undesirable wind or insects.

The rice-paper is not only employed in the *shôji* but also in artificial lighting fixtures, such as the *andon* (lamp) and lanterns; even streetlights have used this material. In contemporary architecture there have been several attempts to introduce paper walls in the design while resolving the problems of fire-proofing and excessive need for repairs. Some consist of inserting the rice-paper between two sheets of glazing. Another way is to keep the *shôji* as a kind of curtain on the inside of a typical glazed wall with metal frame. By doing this the owner can benefit from the *shôji* in good weather, and be protected from cold and fires by a solid transparent wall. However, no modern system is capable of replacing completely the properties of the original, and some say that this is due to the special characteristics of the Japanese mind, trained

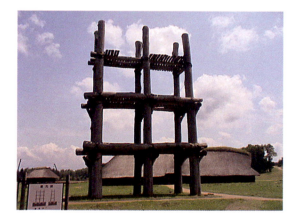

FIGURE 9.1 A watch tower said to have marked the sun's position, reconstructed from the Jômon Era (Some 3000 years ago). The posts of chestnut wood are 15 metres high. Location: Sannai Maruyama (Aomori)

FIGURE 9.2 View of a typical *shôji*

in an elliptical culture where fuzzy vision is often preferable to sharp contrast (Plummer, 1995). This is also the argument of the aforementioned writing by Tanizaki.

Temples

In many sacred buildings the devices used to control solar radiation are even more carefully planned and designed than for dwellings. A well-known case is that of the Karesansui or 'Dry Gardens'. The Karesansui are void spaces treated like a shallow pond filled with rocks and gravel that are set in front of the main hall of a temple. Their principal aim is to help in Zen meditation by offering concentration to the mind. We will not discuss here their many aesthetic or spiritual properties, but we have observed that this type of garden is invariably oriented to the south and that the colour of the sand employed to decorate it is always white or clear. We decided to apply our simulation method to this special compound of reflective surfaces and chose the famous precinct of Ryôanji in Kyôto, made of raked sand with a disposition of fifteen rocks (Figure 9.5).

The temple's southern eaves are exposed to reflected radiation from the white quartz sand. This material is very porous and will not heat up as much as other materials. In summer values of around 8000 lux have been measured on the underside of the roof (Figure 9.6).

We have performed our simulation for a typical summer day with intensities of up to 100,000 lux on the horizontal (Shukuya, 1993). The results (Figure 9.7) agree closely with measurements taken on the site. This simulation proves that the design of the Karesansui

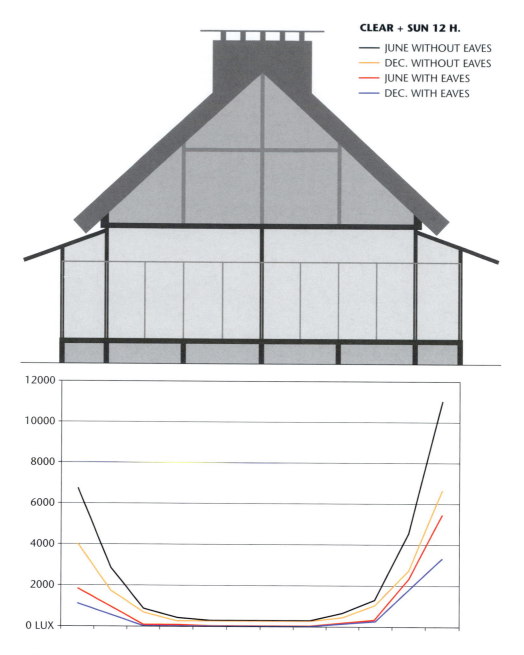

FIGURE 9.3 Model of a popular house called Minka and simulation results. Dimensions of a module: 3.60×7.20m. Lighting levels may reach 4,000 lux near the shôji with eaves, but in the core of the room the intensities are almost negligible

KOBE – DECEMBER 12H – CLEAR + SUN
WITH EAVES

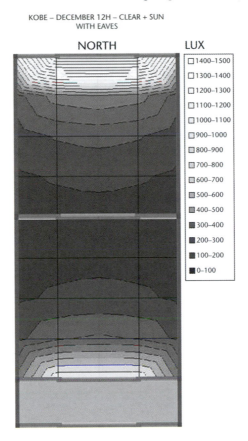

FIGURE 9.4 Lighting distribution in plan with eaves (for 1200 hours in mid-December). The *engawa* and *noki* are very effective in controlling the solar radiation as both façades (north and south) present similar levels around 1400 lux. The soft nature of the oiled paper also helps to reduce glare

FIGURE 9.5 View to the south of the Garden of Ryôanji in Kyôto. Notice the rocks apparently immersed in white gravel and the surrounding walls and trees

FIGURE 9.6 The southern eaves of the temple at Ryôanji with light-coloured wooden rafters

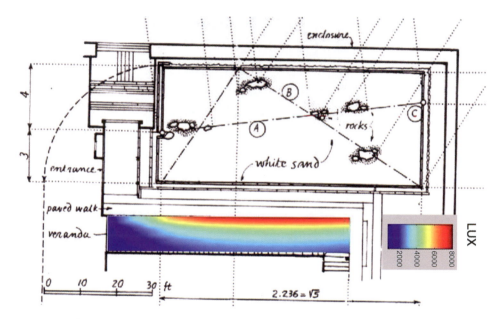

FIGURE 9.7 Radiation field under the roof of the temple of Ryôanji showing an average value of 5000 lux

greatly improves daylighting conditions inside the temple. The colour and orientation of the surface are not random, as the gardens in all other orientations are covered with moss of low albedo. On the other hand, the inclination of the roof reinforces the effect of daylight to the main altar, which is also composed of reflective materials such as mirrors and gold leaf.

Gardens of this type may constitute the first light shelves in history. They come out of a spiritual need for 'enlightenment' (*satori*), but they also enhance physical illumination, and in this near-tropical climate they may be the only way to enhance daylighting as other options such as a skylight would be impractical because of heavy rain and high solar altitudes. On the other hand, this reflection system helps to reduce the limitations of the *shôji* previously described. The Karesansui works equally well in summer and in winter, and it is, indeed, a 'sacred place' because maintenance is difficult and expensive in the middle of the luxuriant vegetation of Japanese woodland.

Another name for Karesansui is Saniwa (Sand Garden), an old denomination of fortune-tellers in the Heian Era. Thus the name suggests that important private ceremonies could have been celebrated there in older times.

Modern evolution

By the end of the nineteenth century, when Japan opened itself again to the world, many of the outstanding environmental features of its buildings were prone to change. Nevertheless, modern architects realized the potential that traditional design solutions had in the contemporary scene. A dramatic effort was made to revitalize features such as those discussed above. One such effort was undertaken by Bruno Taut, a political refugee in Japan from 1933 to 1936, who immediately admitted that:

> the modern Japanese have in their houses a quite right point; the traditional Japanese house can no longer be inhabited by the current people of Japan . . . people who sit in chairs and tables will no more stay crouched under the *kotatsu* wearing several layers of kimonos or remain trembling in the house while the cold winter winds whistle through the rattling *shôji*.

> (Taut, 2003)

Taut devoted himself to the task of finding a modern idiom for the climatic elements of the Japanese house, especially in the aspects of sun and light control and ventilation (Figure 9.8). The high point of this process was his protracted sketch for the façades of the Okura Villa in Tokyo where he incorporated *noki* and *engawa* with a kind of light shelf intended to ensure ventilation in the rainy periods (Figure 9.9).

Taut had started as an industrial design teacher in Japan and his models of lamps and furniture were sold at the Miratiss shop in Tokyo. He was convinced that lighting on the table plane at a Japanese traditional house was inadequate, and his section with increased height and clerestories would contribute to remedy this major drawback, boosting the production or European-style chairs and tables – a curiosity at the time in Japan.

We have simulated this section in winter and in summer to assess its performance (Figure 9.10) and have found it likely that the levels of illuminance would be augmented as compared with the traditional façade when the sun is present. However, under cloudy sky the level of

FIGURE 9.8 Window conceived as a folding screen designed by Bruno Taut at Hyuga House, Atami

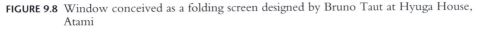

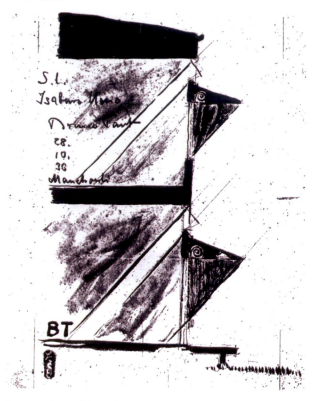

FIGURE 9.9 Sketch for a section of the Okura Villa in Tokyo. Notice the patterns of sun-rays and shadow drawn by Bruno Taut and the case for venetian blinds

Source: Sketch by Bruno Taut from 1936 edition of Japan in Pictures, vol. 4, no. 11

light is very low, and the effect sought by Taut may not have been realized. Even so, he maintained this section in his posthumous projects of 1938 for school buildings in Turkey (Ankara, Trebzon and Izmir).

Another important architect who took great pains to preserve a Japanese light in his projects was the Czech-American Antonin Raymond. Together with his wife, the artist Noemi Pernessin, they established a practice in Japan in 1920 that lasted until 1970 (Figures 9.11 and 9.12). As in the case of Bruno Taut, the Raymonds were always concerned with the use of natural materials adapted to the Japanese climate. In fact, this was the main source of problems in their association with Frank Lloyd Wright for the Imperial Hotel at Tokyo (Raymond, 1973). Antonin Raymond extracted many lessons for his projects from the traditional solutions that he knew so well as a result of his frequent trips and explorations in the country before the Pacific War. But his genius was not restricted to Japan. In 1937, forced by the rise of militarism, he left Japan temporarily but he managed to build an extraordinary compound in Pondicherry (India), the Ashram for the guru Sri Aurobindo (Figure 9.13). Here in two tall blocks of dormitories for the disciples, the first modern brise-soleil (Figure 9.14) appears in all its magnitude. Raymond's drawing explains succinctly that this is a façade intended for buildings in tropical climates.

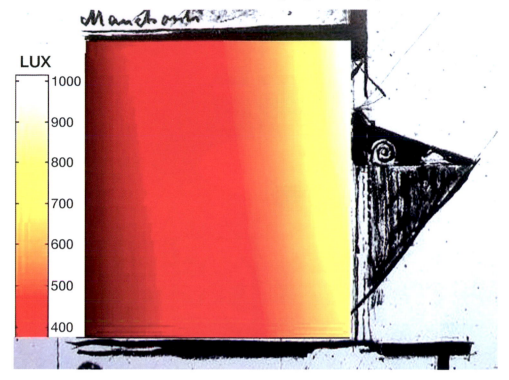

FIGURE 9.10 Summer sectional distribution of daylight at the Okura Villa

Influenced by his intense experiences in Japan, and later at Angkor Wat (Raymond, 1973), Raymond became aware of the importance of shadow and reflected light in Asia, and thus adapted the properties of horizontal 'mirrors' to buildings several storeys high. The performance of such a system was comparable to that of a conventional window.

FIGURE 9.11 The Raymonds at their house and studio at Azabu (Tokyo); notice the wooden columns and the *shôji* window

FIGURE 9.12 A representative work by Raymond, the house for F. Inoue at Takasaki with *shôji*, *andon* lantern and a Japanese garden to the south

Source: Japan Architect 33, 1999

Conclusion

Japanese traditional architecture is unique and truly environmental, and thus Japanese people and their architects have developed a natural sensibility towards lighting features and strategies. This inclination manifests itself in the works of recent artists and creators, but also in forgotten scientists such as Jiro Yamauchi, who in 1932 defined for the first time the concept of photic field (Yamauchi, 1932). This was to be the basis for later works of Higbie, Moon and Spencer among other pioneers of lighting science. Following his theories and example we have striven to demonstrate, with the help of contemporary simulation tools, the efficacy of the solutions that were so inspirational in his work, and that still continue to exert their influence on designers from all countries who approach the question of sunlight with naïve and contemplative eyes. To show the importance of light as a timeless way of expression in the Oriental mind, we would finally like to draw the example of a rare Chinese-Japanese character, which depicts the Sun, the Moon and a Mirror-like object; generally translated as 'Alliance' (Ch. *Meng*; Jp. *Meî*), it suggests a lasting truce with Nature 盟.

FIGURE 9.13 View from the south of the dormitories in the Ashram of Sri Aurobindo, Pondicherry, India; notice the façade covered with blinds made of mineral fibre

FIGURE 9.14 The brise-soleil from the inside of the rooms

Acknowledgements

In this research of twenty years we would like to show appreciation for our Masters, Kenichi Kimura at Waseda and Yuichiro Kodama at Kobe. The Odajima family has always been supportive regardless of how extravagant our research interest may have been. Let peace reign among them. We would like to also thank the librarians at Kobe Design University for their tenacity in helping us to find the long-forgotten Yamauchi papers. Juan F. Ojeda from the University of Seville was instrumental in the preparation of graphs for the section on Bruno Taut.

References

Cabeza-Lainez, J. M. (2006) *Fundamentals of Luminous Radiative Transfer*, Seville, Crowley Editions.
Kojiki, The (1992) *Old Chronicles of Japan*, Tokyo, Tuttle Books.
Plummer, H. (1995) *Light in Japanese Architecture*, Tokyo, A+U.
Raymond, A. (1973) *An Autobiography*, Tokyo, Tuttle Books.
Shukuya, M. (1993) *Hikari to Netsu no Kenchiku Kankyogaku* (The environmentally conscious architecture of light and heat), in Japanese, Tokyo, Maruzen.
Tanizaki, J. (1977) *In Praise of Shadows,* Stony Creek CT, Leete's Island Books.
Taut, B. (2003) *Ich Liebe die Japanische Kultur*, Berlin, Gebr. Mann Verlag.
Yamauchi, J. (1932) 'Theory of field of illumination', *Researches of the Electro-technical Laboratory*, Tokyo, No. 339.

10

INSPIRATION FROM THE VERNACULAR IN THE ARCHITECTURE OF LUIS BARRAGÁN

Anibal Figueroa and Gloria Castorena

Introduction

Luis Barragán said in 1965:

> Before the machine age, even in the centre of cities, nature was a trusted companion, partner of the baker, the ironsmith, the carpenter . . . Nowadays, this situation has been turned around: man can not find nature, not even when he leaves the city to enjoy it. Locked in his shiny automobile, man is within nature a foreign body. A billboard is enough to erase the call of nature. Then nature becomes a fragment of nature and man a fragment of man. The promised dialogue between man and nature becomes a hysterical, monotonous human monologue.
>
> (Smith, 1967)

First of all, Barragán proposed a development of architectural and urban designs that was based on traditional elements. The re-valorization of the so called 'vernacular' architecture is a fundamental element of his projects (Figure 10.1). This is particularly important in our 'modern' and lately 'global' society, which has constantly undervalued traditional solutions, promoting standardized and technologically 'advanced' design for use worldwide.

Second, Barragán's architectural designs consider sensual perception as a key element of spatial experience. His proposals pay particular attention to sun patterns,

MAP 10 Mexico City, Mexico

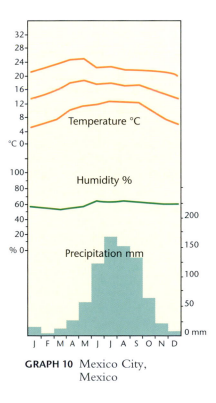

GRAPH 10 Mexico City, Mexico

FIGURE 10.1 At Hacienda Temixco, Morelos, Mexico (seventeenth and eighteenth centuries), the origin of Barragán's interpretation of space, proportion, light, sound and materials is easily recognizable

daylighting, noise control and ventilation. He did not agree with codes that stipulate minimum levels of comfort for these parameters. Instead, he used his personal intuition and perception to manipulate the physical factors and achieve a carefully balanced equilibrium between physical conditions and built environment. Instead of complex computer models, Barragán followed an empirical approach. He made careful observations in other buildings and then translated the principles to suit his own work. He would design in sketches, then move to large-size paper models and finally build and modify the idea as many times as necessary. Construction was a slow and careful full-size model, which was shaped and reshaped until the desired sensual perception was completed. Barragán developed a school of thought that Kenneth Frampton defined as 'critical regionalism', based on the idea of a regional attitude towards design (Frampton, 1975). For Barragán, a design must take into account its physical and climatic conditions as well as its cultural background. He designed only for places for which he knew the climate and habits of the inhabitants. How to differentiate design criteria for a specific region is a fundamental issue of an energy-conscious design. Barragán's architectural masterpieces are brilliant examples of this principle. However, his approach to traditional design is based on the ability of the architect to identify the essential building elements and then to 'convert' them into a contemporary image. His architecture is far removed from the 'picturesque' or the historic conservationist approach. In Barragán's words 'all historic architecture was revolutionary and contemporary on its days' (Barragán, 1986). Therefore, we need a contemporary expression that uses and revitalizes the knowledge from previous generations.

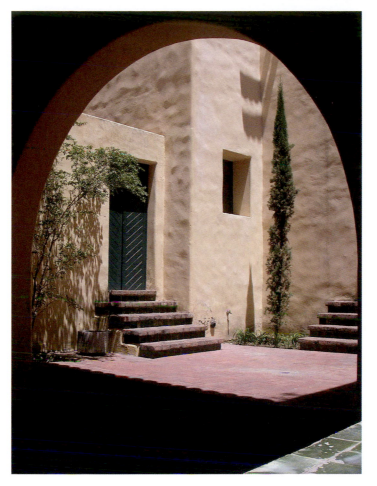

FIGURE 10.2 At one of Barragán's earliest designs (Casa Gonzalez Luna, 1928) traditional elements are combined into contemporary design

His designs recover ancient constructive methods and finishing materials, emphasizing their optical and thermal qualities. Barragán insisted that we should not assume that all new technology is good and disdain old technologies as obsolete, because old constructive methods have acquired an intrinsic empirical value over many generations and have been tested for specific weather conditions and material resources (Figure 10.2). Additionally, the old master masons, carpenters, ironsmiths and other craftsmen are inheritors of a centuries-old knowledge.

Light and sun

Natural light

Barragán's designs pay a great deal of attention to daylighting. According to his ideas, natural light gives spaces a different character at different times of the day and year. He planned to control both the quantity and quality of natural light. This was achieved by extensive use of large-scale models that were professionally photographed. This stage was always preliminary, allowing for options to be evaluated and new ideas tested. As the building was constructed, he supervised the construction daily, modifying many of the openings (Figueroa, 2002). Natural light – direct and indirect – was a much sought after source for special effects. The character of a space was given by the admission of natural light. At times, dimly lit spaces were intentionally produced as a transition from the outside to the interior. On other occasions, darkened spaces were provided as places for rest or meditation.

Colour temperature

On Barragán's buildings, the selection of colour was always left for the end. Most of the interior walls were painted white. It was for special areas of the building that intense colours were used, such as pink, yellow or orange. Even those colours were first tested on large 1×1m paper boards. Once some choices were made, a 'full scale' test was carried out by painting all the walls and – if necessary – repainting them as many times as needed.

Barragán found an effect that can be described as 'coloured light'. It is clear that coloured glass has been used for centuries, particularly as stained glass windows for decoration. However, Barragán used the same principle in a completely different way. He usually hid the light source and then painted the glass, mixing 'warm' light with planes lit by 'cold' light. The result was a mixture that changed the indoor quality of space and our perception of colour. He achieved spectacular effects by the use of simple devices such as painted or stained glass, reflective grids, trellises, etc. that ranged from a warm yellow and orange – generally used for its association with sunshine – to cold purple-blue openings (Figure 10.3).

Lighting levels

Barragán understood that not all activities or individuals required the same amount of light. Although building codes set minimum lighting levels, he often sought to achieve lower levels, either by using small openings, or by providing the means for darkening rooms totally or in a controlled way:

> The day is luminous and the night is dark, we must allow spaces to be that way. Each time of the day has its own beauty in light or in its absence. It is a mistake to try to turn the night into day.
>
> (Figueroa, 1980)

Artificial lighting

In Barragán's architecture there is an absence of ceiling lamps. Most electric light is by lamps placed close to the floor or attached to furniture. In this way, walls and their texture are strongly perceived and ceilings are lit softly and evenly by indirect lighting. Other light sources included table lamps located in most spaces of the house. The architect used them as accent and working light. By reducing artificial lighting to a minimum, Barragán made efficient and selective use of electric appliances. He derived this principle by aiming to convey to spaces a sense of mystery, intimacy, enclosure and relaxation. This was accomplished by lowering both natural and artificial lighting levels and by controlling the direction of light sources.

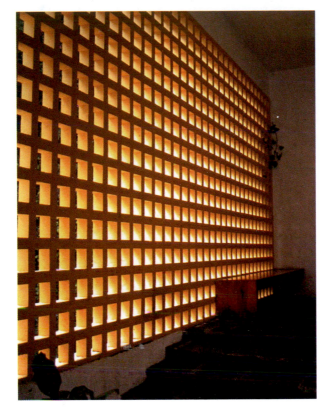

FIGURE 10.3 Las Capuchinas Convent (1955) is a good example of colour temperature. The yellow grid produces an effect of sunshine even on cloudy days

Sun patterns

Sun movements were carefully considered in all projects as they cast shadows or allowed the direct beam through windows. This can be observed at the Gilardi House (Barragán, 1976), where the swimming pool-dining space is brightly lit by a sun ray admitted by a high window at the end of a long promenade. There, a 'slice' of sun is allowed into a corner of the room. Its window source is hidden, so that we become surprised by a moving light that reflects, diffracts and illuminates the water surface and the space. Any wave on the surface of the pool produces a dynamic sun pattern on the walls and ceiling (Figure 10.4).

Dialogue: man–nature

Climatic conditions

In the mild and temperate climatic conditions of central Mexico, Barragán was one of the very few contemporary architects to use terraces, porticoes and roof areas as important spaces in a house design. He understood that for this climate the use of the outdoor and semi-open spaces was most desirable. Barragán's houses spread into the outdoors through windows and

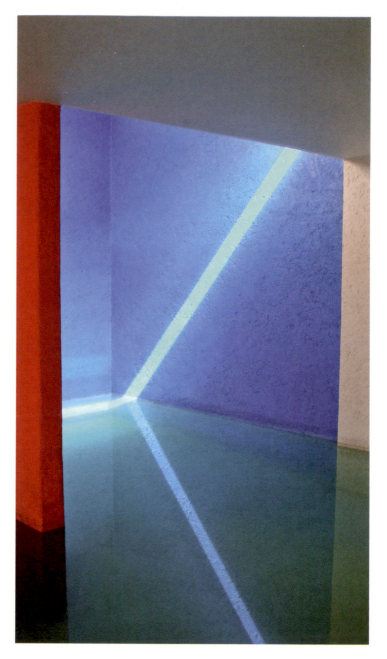

FIGURE 10.4 The pool and dining room area of the Casa Gilardi (1976) is a sun path experiment: reflecting, diffracting and casting its light

porticoes. They usually have a semi-covered terrace as their most privileged space. It is used to eat, relax or play. At the same time, this space is an observation deck for weather and nature.

The outdoor space

In part due to Barragán, external spaces such as patios and gardens found new uses in contemporary Mexican architecture. His concepts about green space, terraces, porticoes, fountains and many other outdoor elements contributed to a more 'natural' approach to architecture. His influence can be recognized in a large number of buildings in Mexico and in other places as distant as Europe or Japan (Figure 10.5).

Urban concepts

Instead of destroying and imposing urban and landscape concepts, Barragán's designs started from what was on site. His urban concepts also included plazas, promenades, hidden fountains and parks (Figure 10.6). Existing trees and contours defined the final shape of a design. Water was always present to refresh people and animals and cool down the dry air of Mexico's central plateau. Urban pavements were defined with precision in order to provide textures and create a comfortable surface in terms of heat and light.

FIGURE 10.5 El Campanario Fountain (1964) shows how Barragán controls the environmental qualities of outdoor space through trees, walls and water effects

FIGURE 10.6 Jardines del Pedregal de San Angel subdivision (1942–56): here, nature and urban planning are combined

Natural ventilation and noise control

All of Barragán's designs considered natural ventilation and solar exposure as means for acclimatizing indoor spaces. None of his houses had air conditioning or mechanical heating. Careful attention was paid to window orientation. Most of the glazing surfaces were oriented towards the east and south. They were always recessed or protected by trellises with plants or flowers.

Chimneys had a dual function: they were used for natural ventilation on warm days and as a heat source in cold weather (Figure 10.7). The stack effect produced a constant air movement that ventilated effectively the main spaces of the houses. In Barragán's designs silence and noise control are a primary element. Walls and windows were designed to reduce outside noises, while also maintaining a direct link with the outdoors. Some of the windows were fixed; ventilation was provided by the chimneys, a few operable openings and small electric fans. Louis Kahn said in relation to Louis Barragán's house that 'silence, like a music, fills the house' (Kahn, 1984).

FIGURE 10.7 Chimneys ventilate or heat the large public area in Luis Barragán's house in Tacubaya (1945)

Conclusion

It is most important to learn from Barragán that a good architectural interior, landscape or urban concept will always take into account the passive and low energy aspects. An approach rooted on traditional architecture, spaces and materials can be contemporary. If set apart from fashion, architecture must aim to be timeless. A good passive and low-energy design must attend to all senses to enrich our perception of nature and environment. It is relevant to study Luis Barragán's architecture from these points of view, because they demonstrate that passive architecture can be very pleasant and should have greater value and more virtues than an ordinary building.

Acknowledgements

This document is part of a large research effort on Luis Barragán's designs that has been supported by the Universidad Autonoma Metropolitana, The Fundación Casa Barragán, The Fundación de Arquitectura Tapatía, the Barragán's Foundation, the National Council for the Culture and Arts (CONACULTA, Mexico) and numerous individuals that include past and present owners of his private work. We thank them all for their encouragement and endorsement.

References

Barragán, L. (1986) *Barragán*, México City, Museo Rufino Tamayo, p.128.

Figueroa, A. (1980) Notes from an interview of Anibal Figueroa with Luis Barragán, unpublished.

Figueroa, A. (2002) *El Arte de Ver Con Inocencia: Platicas con Luis Barragán*, México City, Universidad Autonoma Metropolitana (UAM), p.56.

Frampton, K. (1975) *A History of Modern Architecture*, New York, Penguin Architectural Books, p.356.

Kahn, L. (1984) *What has been will always be*, New York, Rizzoli, p.831.

Smith, C. (1967) *Builders in the Sun: Five Mexican Architects*, New York, Architectural Press, p.76.

11

THE NEW VERNACULAR OF SEVERIANO PORTO IN THE AMAZON

Leticia Neves

MAP 11 Manaus, Brazil

The architect Severiano Porto

Severiano Porto was the pioneer architect who actuated these principles in the Amazonian region by using new ideas of space treatment according to the environment and by giving attention to important aspects of the regional architecture. The idea of bioclimatic architecture frequently appears in the architect's works, and encompasses adjusting the building to the region's climate, materials, processes and local conditions, showing concern for the integration of construction and nature. With his work in the Amazonian region, Porto heads the group of Brazilian architects who diffused a regionalized approach to architecture throughout the country in the 1960s. Together with his partner, Mario Emilio Ribeiro, he built most of his works in the Amazon region, especially in the city of Manaus, where he lived and worked for thirty-six years. The region, which has plenty of native forest, demanded a close relationship with the environment. It was by trying to establish this relationship that Porto searched – right from the outset of his work – for a deep contact with climate, society and local culture, which enormously enriched what he produced: 'without excluding his own background, the architect began a long and loving apprenticeship of the Amazonian way of life' (Segawa, 1993). A large part of this involvement resulted from the contact Porto established with the local population, the *caboclo*. Based on empirical knowledge, they had a lot to teach him about local materials and construction methods.

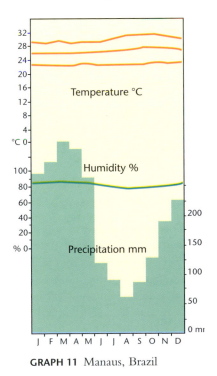

GRAPH 11 Manaus, Brazil

The bioclimatic issue was always a priority in his work. His architecture is called 'Amazonian' because it strives to deal with all the peculiarities of the region, mostly of resources and specialized labour. In Porto's definition of architecture these intentions become clear:

> Architecture is a group of factors that are interlaced and grouped according to the needs of a programme, *the specific conditions of a site*, *the resources of its region*, its *environmental conditions*, *technology* to be used, ancient, *regional*, and all other existent in the epoch, financial possessions, etc. All the factors transformed in space in a sensible, logical, technical and beautiful manner. (emphasis added)
>
> (Porto, 2005)

Use of timber

When Porto arrived in the Brazilian Amazon, the region had very few professionals in the construction field, and the idea of adapting a building to local conditions was almost non-existent. The architect put in question the architecture that was being produced at the time, which followed the Modernism of architectural magazines and was distant from local reality. He introduced new patterns and construction methods, always searching for a better way to integrate architecture and nature. The use of timber was a natural choice. It was easy to obtain, easily manipulated by local labourers and suitable for the local climate. It was by observing the inhabitants in their own habitat that Severiano noticed the importance of timber and local techniques, since they were adjusted to the specific circumstances of the region. However, before Porto started working with timber, the material had been used only for the precarious construction of popular habitation. The architect demonstrated that timber was a noble material, that it was suited to the local reality and that it could be used on buildings of quality by constructing his own house in timber: 'We must adopt solutions that consider solar radiation, wind, rain, our labour conditions, the building material, and there we include the timber, plenty and abundant in our forests' (Porto, 1971).

Two of Porto's main works on which the use of timber was explored both aesthetically and structurally are analysed here: the architect's residence, completed in 1971 (Porto, 1982), and the Balbina Centre for Environmental Protection, built between 1983 and 1988 (Porto and Ribeiro, 1989). The paper presents the architectural solutions used to adapt these buildings to the hot and humid weather of the region, emphasizing the strategies for achieving thermal comfort.

Architect's residence, 1971

The house needed to be built rapidly, in about six months, and at low cost. Timber was cheap, easily available and well known to local builders. The architect could reduce construction cost by 25 per cent compared to social housing built by the government for low income families (Gagliardi, 1967–68). An important objective was to have a minimum impact on the environment, by considering from the outset the specific conditions of the site, situated near a rivulet, and aiming for maximum integration with the surrounding vegetation. The two-storey house has its structure in *sucupira* and *maçaranduba* timber (local species) with concrete used only on bathroom floors. Ceramic and timber cover the floors. The roof is finished in asbestos-cement tiles. The ground-floor plan accommodates an internal garden surrounded by the living areas. The upper-floor contains two bedrooms and the office. There is close contact with the outside through the open planning and this gives a sense of unity between house and terrain (Figures 11.1, 11.2 and 11.3).

Bioclimatic strategies

The house presents creative solutions for providing thermal comfort. The use of large overhangs and verandas along the west façade attenuates the unfavourable orientation. A fixed panel made of horizontal louvres above the garage (east façade) acts as a shading device, protecting from rain as well as obstructing solar radiation, but without inhibiting air circulation. Perforated panels are also used to ventilate the attic space, which is composed of a timber ceiling and the asbestos-cement roof. The existing vegetation of the terrain was well preserved and helps to maintain a more stable microclimate (Figures 11.4 and 11.5).

The asbestos-cement tile gets darker in a short period of time, due to the hot-humid weather and fungal growth, resulting in a higher absorption of solar radiation and consequent transmission of heat, by radiation, to the ceiling and the indoor area. As was observed by Givoni:

> Lightweight roofs, covered with tiles or sheets of asbestos-cement or aluminium, are preferable in a warm-wet climate owing to their low heat capacity. But such roofs, which are externally usually dark in colour, or at any rate, not whitewashed, are heated by solar radiation and may cause heat stress during the daytime.
>
> (Givoni, 1976)

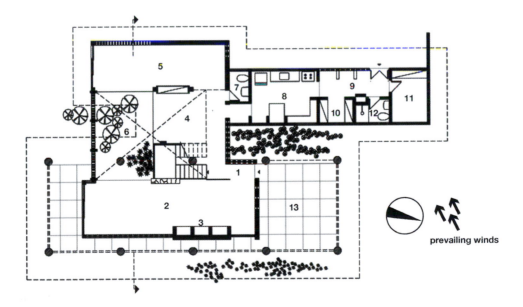

prevailing winds

FIGURE 11.1 Ground-floor plan. Note: 1. hall, 2. living room, 3. bar, 4. dining room, 5. veranda, 6. internal garden, 7. toilet, 8. kitchen, 9. laundry, 10. storage, 11. maid's room, 12. bathroom, 13. garage

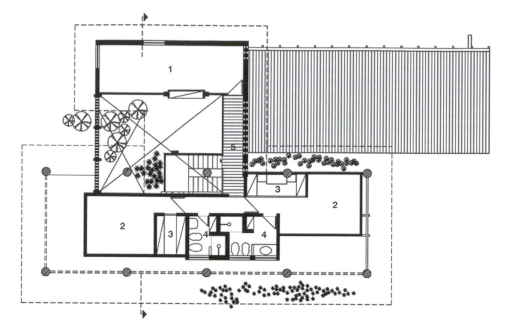

FIGURE 11.2 First-floor plan. Note: 1. living room, 2. bedroom, 3. wardrobe, 4. bathroom, 5. passage

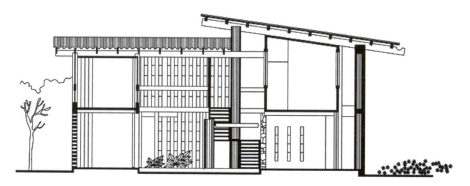

FIGURE 11.3 Transversal section

The protection from solar radiation by vegetation is of great importance, and helps improve the internal microclimate of the residence. The internal garden also contributes to this. Some of the external walls are of perforated concrete blocks (*cobogos*) commonly used throughout Brazil. They allow the house to be permanently open to the prevailing north-east winds. The ground level is also fitted with vertical windows glazed with yellow glass to provide more luminous comfort to the interior. The result is a permanently ventilated space around the internal garden (Figure 11.6).

Most external walls are of timber. This ensures a low thermal capacity preventing heat accumulation during daytime. Some of the internal walls are of stone, a heavyweight material, which is more appropriate for heat storage where appropriate (Figure 11.7).

FIGURE 11.4 General view

Source: Severiano Porto

FIGURE 11.5 View of east façade

Source: Hugo Segawa

FIGURE 11.6 Internal garden, surrounded by concrete perforated elements

Source: Hugo Segawa

FIGURE 11.7 Living room, with wall made of stone

Source: Severiano Porto

In the bedrooms, horizontal wooden shingles and adjustable shutters provide satisfactory control over solar gain while allowing cross-ventilation. The residence received a prize from the Brazilian Architects' Institute for using timber in an appropriate manner, according to the climate and the environment, becoming an example of architecture harmoniously introduced in the regional context: '[an] excellent idea from the author, consistent, elaborated with Brazilian vocabulary [. . .] without being alienated by the contemporary techniques'. (Campos, 2003)

Balbina Centre for Environmental Protection, 1983–1988

The Balbina Centre for Environmental Protection is situated in the city of Presidente Figueiredo, near Manaus. It is a remarkable building that occupies an exceptional place in Brazilian architecture. The construction presents singular and creative solutions:

> Severiano Porto and Mario Emilio Ribeiro's work is remarkable for many reasons, but mostly for the sensitive and sophisticated use of wood in all its potentialities and for the easy elegance with which the various spaces are arranged under the beautiful continuous roof.
>
> (Segawa, 1991)

Balbina is a hydroelectric power station built in the 1980s to provide energy to the city of Manaus. Porto was called upon to design the building at the centre, which was to house the people responsible for studying the effects of the hydroelectric power station on

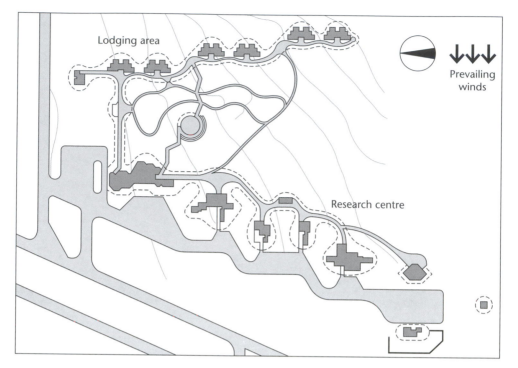

FIGURE 11.8 Site plan

FIGURE 11.9 General view

Source: Severiano Porto

the eco-system, taking into account the environmental impacts such an undertaking would cause in the forest, and to climate, fauna and flora, etc. The centre would be responsible for studying ways to reduce to a minimum the damage to the environment. Since a very large area would be flooded, part of the forest would be drowned, so the architect was free to use as much wood for the construction as he wanted, from the various species and types that existed in the area. Porto worked with timber in a completely free way, using it in several different forms: trunks, rectangular columns and beams, planks and boards. The building was meant to comprise two blocks: a research centre, with laboratories and spaces to collect data, and a lodging area. Only the research centre was built (Figures 11.8 and 11.9).

Bioclimatic strategies

To cover the roof Porto used a regional type of tile called *cavaco* (shingles made of splintered wood) that was produced on site by local builders (Figure 11.10). According to the architect, the *cavaco* gives greater formal freedom than the common ceramic tile, since it can accommodate any kind of design including curved forms. It also has advantages over straw – a material frequently used in the region – because of its higher durability.

The roof is a continuous and unique surface that covers the whole complex, varying in form, height and width, providing good protection from solar radiation and rain. Under this envelope, the building is adapted to the natural slope of the terrain. Spaces are located according to the prevailing winds, which are east–west, in different levels, connected by ramps and protected by the wide overhangs of the roof (Figure 11.11).

FIGURE 11.10 View of the roof, covered with *cavaco* tiles

Source: Severiano Porto

FIGURE 11.11 Covered pathways

Source: Severiano Porto

FIGURE 11.12 Openings for stack ventilation

Source: Severiano Porto

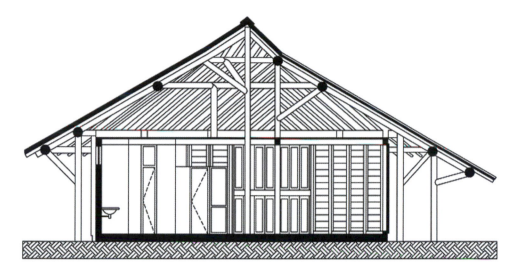

FIGURE 11.13 Transversal section

Brick walls and timber ceilings enclose the spaces under the roof. Some of the laboratories that depend on close control of temperature and humidity have air conditioning. These rooms have skylights, through which the structure of the roof can be observed. The other rooms depend on cross-ventilation, provided by openings on both the windward and the leeward sides of the building, and on stack ventilation, provided by openings in the roof (Figure 11.12). Between the roof and the ceiling there is a ventilated attic space that ensures better thermal comfort to indoor areas. The distance between roof and ceiling reaches eight metres at the highest points (Figure 11.13).

In his career Severiano Porto undertook almost 200 projects, most of them in the 1970s and 1980s. In 2001, after thirty-six years in the Amazonian region, Porto left Manaus and returned to Rio de Janeiro.

Acknowledgement

The author would like to thank Professor Rosana Caram and Fapesp for the support given to this research.

References

Campos, E. R. (2003) 'A arquitetura brasileira de Severiano Mário Porto', *Arquitextos*, no 209, December. Available at: www.vitruvius.com.br/arquitextos/arq000/esp209.asp (accessed 10 March 2004).

Gagliardi, V. B. (1967–68) 'Arquitetura brasileira do ano', *ABA-GB*, Rio de Janeiro, pp.80–125.

Givoni, B. (1976) *Man, Climate and Architecture*, second edition, London, Applied Science Publishers Ltd.

Neves, S. (2005) 'Interview with Severiano Porto', 30 March.

Porto, S. (1971) 'Severiano Porto: entrevista', *Bom Dia*, year 1, no 3, 31 March, pp.30–34.

Porto, S. (1982) 'Arquitetura tropical na residência de Severiano Porto, em Manaus', *Projeto*, São Paulo, no 40, May, p.22–25.

Porto, S. and Ribeiro, M. E. (1989) 'Centro de proteção ambiental de Balbina', *Projeto*, São Paulo, no 125, September, pp.69–75.

Segawa, H. (1991) 'Centro di protezione ambientale in Amazzonia', *Spazio e Società*, Firenze, no 56, October/December, pp.34–41.

Segawa, H. (1993) 'Severiano Porto: la sfida dell'Amazzonia', *Spazio e Società,* Firenze, no 61, January/March, pp.8–17.

12

COMPARISON OF TRADITIONAL THAI HOUSES WITH CONTEMPORARY DESIGNS

Kevin McCartney, Paruj Antarikananda and Elena Douvlou

MAP 12 Bangkok, Thailand

Introduction

The practice of drawing on traditional architecture to inform contemporary design has been promoted by many theorists and distinguished architects such as Hassan Fathy (Steele, 1988). Among other advantages they claim is the benefit to be derived from centuries of experience in adapting form and material selection to achieve comfort in relation to the local climate. As much as 15 per cent of the book *The climatic dwelling* is devoted to a section titled 'Tradition' (Cofaigh et al., 1996). A notable critic of this concept is Rapoport (1969). He argued against the concept, which he termed *environmental determinism*. He thought that people might be seriously misled if they attributed the forms and materials adopted in traditional buildings solely to the physical environment. To support his argument he demonstrated examples of buildings in which cultural and religious values had clearly dominated over rational climatic responses in determining such features as orientation and the size and position of windows and doors.

Rapoport's work introduced a note of caution for those advocating the process of drawing inspiration for bioclimatic design from the regional architecture of the past. Others have drawn attention to the way in which changes in available technology and user needs affect radical changes in the development of the stereotypes designers use in formulating appropriate formal solutions to design problems (Hawkes, 1996).

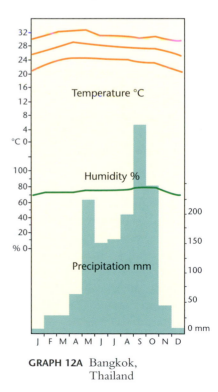

GRAPH 12A Bangkok, Thailand

In order to counter the tendency to borrow naively from tradition, this study addresses a fundamental question: do traditional Thai houses perform better than a typical contemporary Thai house in creating comfortable internal conditions? If they do, this would lend support to the 'learning from tradition' approach. If the contemporary house performs better than the traditional designs, it is important to recognize why this might be happening, and to adapt the tradition-based approach accordingly.

Method

The method adopted was the use of numerical simulation rather than field measurements. It should be noted that the focus is on the building form and materials; there is no sophisticated modelling of user responses. The environmental analysis program Ecotect from Square One was used to predict the performance of house designs in different regional climates in Thailand. Three zones of Thailand were selected for this study, from a more comprehensive analysis by Antarikananda (2005).

Comfort indicators

The cooling loads are significantly higher than the heating loads, with the exception of the traditional house in the south zone, where both heating and cooling loads are relatively very small. Therefore the response to the threat of overheating was taken as the primary indicator of the success of the house design in responding to climate. Three indicators of response to overheating are used: (1) duration of overheating; (2) intensity of overheating, measured in degree-hours/year; (3) cooling load, which is an estimate of the useful energy required to keep the internal temperatures within the comfort zone.

Regional climates

The simulation exercises were carried out using climatic data from three regions (Thai Meteorological Department, undated) considered to be distinctive and representative of the range of conditions encountered in the country. The southern region is the peninsula bounded by the Andaman Sea on the west and the South China Sea to the east. The central region is largely a coastal plain, extending from the northern end of the peninsula to Chai Nat, and includes the capital, Bangkok. The north-eastern region is a high level plateau that has borders with Laos to the north and east, and with Cambodia to the south. Climate data from Songklha was used to represent the southern region as humid with high daytime temperatures. Bangkok data represented the central region, with lower humidity than the south, but with higher temperatures. The climate of Ubon Ratchathani, with humidity generally lower than both other zones and a wider range of temperatures, represented the north-eastern region. The comfort zone for each region was calculated using the Weather Tool in Ecotect. This attempts to account for acclimatization by relating the comfort zone to the annual average temperature. Both the southern and the north-eastern regions have comfort zones defined between 24.5 and 29.5°C, while the hotter central zone has a comfort zone defined between 25.5 and 30.5°C.

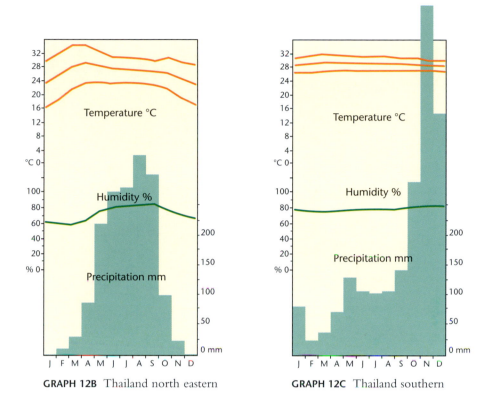

GRAPH 12B Thailand north eastern

GRAPH 12C Thailand southern

House types for analysis

The contemporary house, shown in Figure 12.1, is constructed with concrete structure and floors, brick walls and a plaster board ceiling with 3cm of insulation and concrete tiles on the roof. The windows are single glazed. This was taken to be typical of houses currently being built in all regions of Thailand.

Scholars have suggested that there are four regionally distinct house types in Thailand. The regional differences can be attributed to climate, resources, technology, culture and beliefs (Warren, 1983). The traditional houses selected for comparison with the contemporary house in the south, central, and north-east regions of the country are illustrated in Figures 12.2, 12.3 and 12.4. They are constructed almost entirely of wood, with clay tiled roofs, and no ceilings. There is no glass in the window apertures. Detailed descriptions are available (Office of the National Culture Commission, n.d.).

Results

Temperatures in the contemporary house are too high for longer periods than those in the traditional houses in all three regions (Figure 12.5). Therefore, if there is no mechanical means of controlling the internal environment, the traditional house will be comfortable for longer periods than the contemporary house in all analysed climatic regions of Thailand. This is

FIGURE 12.1 Typical contemporary house in Thailand

probably due to the higher ventilation rates associated with unglazed fenestration, and lower thermal mass in the traditional houses built with timber.

In the south and central zones, not only is the duration of overheating greater in the contemporary house but the intensity is also greater (Figure 12.6). The cooling degree-hours in the contemporary house are greater than those in the traditional houses. The difference between the traditional and contemporary designs is particularly marked in the central zone. This might be attributed to the increased solar gain through the larger apertures, the use of glass to fill the openings, and the decreased proportion of shading in the contemporary design.

In the north-eastern zone by contrast, although the duration of the overheated period in the contemporary house is longer, the intensity is lower, with the cooling degree-hours in the contemporary house calculated as 53 per cent of those experienced in the traditional house. In this climate the contemporary house benefits from the massive construction in a region where night temperatures often drop below the comfort zone, and there is a larger diurnal temperature swing.

The cooling load is somewhat lower in the contemporary house than in the traditional houses in the central and north-eastern zones (Figure 12.7). In considering cooling loads, the exception is in the south zone where the traditional house cooling load is smaller than that of the contemporary house. The ambient temperatures in the southern zone are influenced by the proximity of the sea, and it appears that the combination of shade and air movement are almost sufficient to keep internal temperatures within the comfort zone. The southern region traditional house has large, vertical apertures that increase natural ventilation. These are protected from the sun by large roof overhangs.

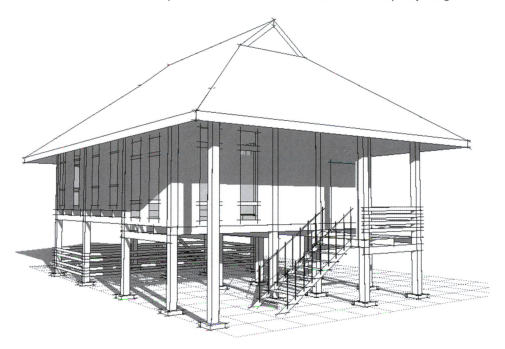

Original Plan

Kitchen   Living room

Bedroom 1   Bedroom 2

FIGURE 12.2a and 12.2b Traditional house, south region of Thailand

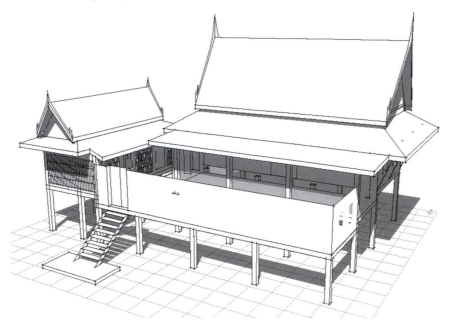

FIGURE 12.3 Traditional house, central region of Thailand

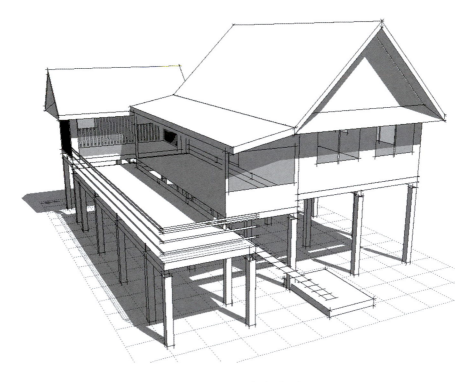

FIGURE 12.4 Traditional house, north-east region of Thailand

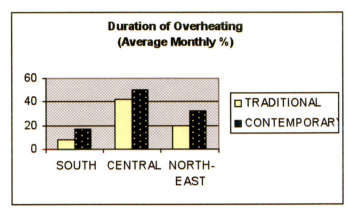

FIGURE 12.5 Comparison of the duration of overheating in a contemporary house and traditional houses from different climatic zones in Thailand

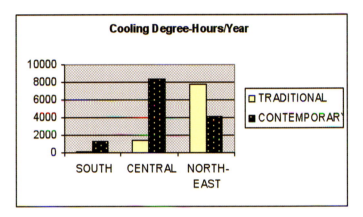

FIGURE 12.6 Comparison of the intensity of overheating in a contemporary house and traditional houses from different climatic zones in Thailand

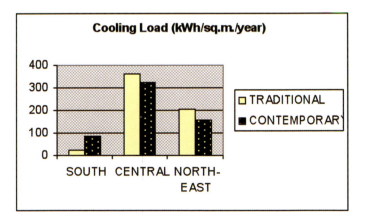

FIGURE 12.7 Comparison of cooling loads in a contemporary house and traditional houses from different climatic zones in Thailand

The cooling load is an indicator of the amount of useful energy required to keep the internal temperatures below the upper level of the comfort zone. Hence Figure 12.7 indicates that, with the exception of the southern zone, the contemporary house will require less energy to achieve comfort if mechanical cooling systems are installed. The higher heat gain, due to both ventilation and conduction through the fabric of the traditional houses, are the probable cause of their inferior performance with respect to cooling load.

Conclusions

In these comparative analyses, the simplest indicator of overheating, the duration of periods when temperatures are too high, provides some evidence to support the proposition that the traditional house designs are superior to the contemporary in providing thermal comfort for all three climatic zones. This supports the argument that traditional architecture is indeed well adapted to the climatic variations across Thailand, and can provide longer periods of thermal comfort when houses are operating in a purely passive mode.

However, the calculation of the cooling degree-hours and the cooling loads reveal a more complex picture. Particularly in the north-east, but also in the central zone, the contemporary house design offers advantages. These advantages would be most apparent in situations where residents wished to install some form of mechanical cooling. This finding is of special interest in the context of changes in the availability of contemporary technologies, lifestyles and user expectations. These changes are leading to increased heat gains within the home and possibly a reduction in the degree of adaptation to high domestic temperatures.

We can conclude that the traditional housing of Thailand does provide useful indicators of appropriate architectural design responses to climate, particularly in the context of purely passive environmental control. However, judicious selectivity is required in deriving lessons from traditional houses, in the design of housing for contemporary clients, using increasing amounts of electrical equipment in the home and using, or aspiring to use, mechanical cooling to extend the period of thermal comfort.

Recommendations

Although the simulation studies did not test these recommendations, it is our conjecture that selected features from traditional housing offer potential improvements to contemporary house designs. Specifically, improved shading, adjustable openings in the form of windows and ventilators, raised platforms and variation in the size of windows in response to the climatic region and the house orientation are likely to improve thermal performance. In the north-east, where there is a more pronounced period when occupants might feel too cold, there may be benefits from incorporating adjustable openings in the building envelope to increase occupant control of ventilation. In the southern region longer roof overhangs are required to increase shading for the contemporary house. In the central region the massive construction of the contemporary house does not appear to offer any advantage in terms of moderating the impact of high ambient temperatures. Houses for the central region would also benefit from improved shading, particularly on the south-west and west façades. The inadequacy of the shading on the west elevation of the typical contemporary house is illustrated in Figure 12.8 (left side). In contrast the adjacent (improved) design shown in Figure 12.8 achieves much more effective shading. It illustrates the incorporation of a number of recommended

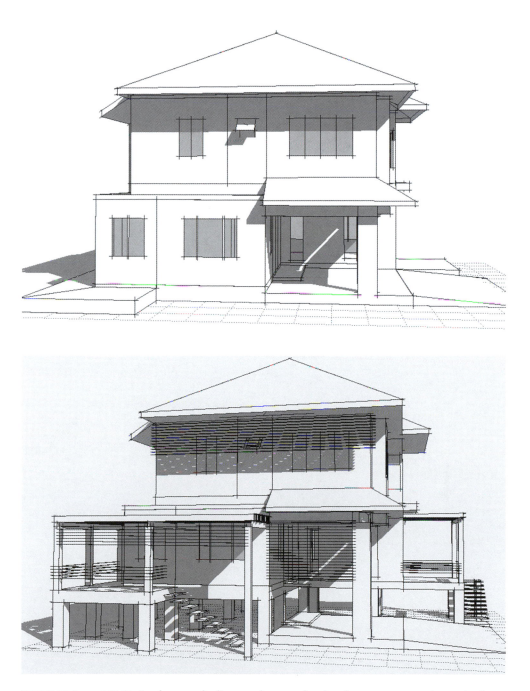

FIGURE 12.8a and 12.8b Inadequate shading on the west façade of a contemporary house in the central region at 3pm in June (top). Below is an improved contemporary design featuring additional shading, raised floors and shaded external platforms

improvements for the contemporary house. The house is raised on columns to avoid flood damage and improve the potential for natural ventilation. There are several projections from the central block, which provide short cross-ventilation routes. A number of roofed verandas are added to provide additional functional space and shading for the apertures in the walls behind them.

References

Antarikananda, Paruj (2005) 'Climate responsive design: recommendation for contemporary house design in Thailand', unpublished MSc thesis, EDAM, University of Portsmouth, UK.

Cofaigh, E., Olley, J. and Lewis, O. (1996) *The Climatic Dwelling*, London, James & James, pp.19–42.

Hawkes, D. (1996) *The Environmental Tradition*, London, Chapman & Hall, pp.46–55.

Office of the National Culture Commission (n.d.) *Thai house of the Central Plain*; available at: www.thailandlife.com/thai-culture/thai-house-of-the-central-plain.html (accessed 13 April 2013).

Rapaport, A. (1969) *House, Form and Culture*, Englewood Cliffs NJ, Prentice Hall.

Steele, J. (1988) *Hassan Fathy*, Architectural Monographs 13, London, Academy Editions.

Thai Meteorological Department (n.d.) 'Climate of Thailand', available at: www.tmd.go.th/en/ (accessed 13 April 2013).

Warren, W. (1989) *Living in Thailand*, London, Thames & Hudson.

13

ENVIRONMENTALLY RESPONSIVE ARCHITECTURE FOR RURAL NORTHERN IRELAND

Joy-Anne Fleming

MAP 13 Belfast, Northern Ireland, UK

Introduction

Northern Ireland is part of the United Kingdom, governed by Great Britain. It is a small country consisting of six of the nine counties of the historic Irish province of Ulster. Ireland has a long history of tenant farming, and an assessment of the current status of housing in Northern Ireland shows that more than a third of the population live rurally, and this continues to increase.[1] The Irish cottage was the autonomous house for rural Northern Ireland from the seventeenth to the nineteenth century. Its form enhanced the beautiful Irish landscape and provided a holistic response to the occupants' requirements. The goal of this study was to design a contemporary alternative that would meet the expected comfort levels of the twenty-first century, but with lower energy consumption than current standard housing. The clients are now the only permanent residents in their large, rural family home, so they would like a house that meets their new lifestyle requirements. They have requested a design that respects, but does not mimic, local architecture, and instead draws from the past yet represents the future. The design was developed through studies of the vernacular, deriving a series of design guidelines from the environmental attributes of traditional architecture. The culmination of the study is a design that incorporates traditional and contemporary design and construction.

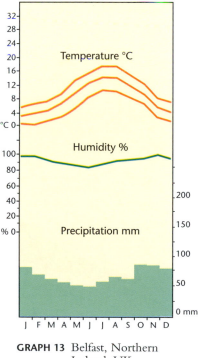

GRAPH 13 Belfast, Northern Ireland, UK

Climate

The geographic latitude of the site is 54°39′N. The air temperature can fall to −4°C and rise to 24°C; however, the average remains between 3°C and 14°C (Figure 13.1). The daily fluctuations are a maximum of 5°C in winter and 10°C in summer.[2]

The annual average relative humidity is 90 per cent. Ireland is one of the windiest parts of Europe with the prevailing wind from the south-west following the Gulf Stream off the Atlantic Ocean.[3] As the site lies in a valley that runs along a north–south axis, the valley channels the wind directly from the south. Local knowledge supports this and confirms that the less frequent north-easterly winds that come in from northern Europe are actually the coldest.[4]

In this climate solar radiation has significant seasonal variations. Lowest irradiance is in December, with averages up to $100W/m^2$ on the horizontal and a maximum of $260W/m^2$; the highest is in May with an average of $420W/m^2$ and a maximum of $880W/m^2$. The low sun angle in winter permits direct solar radiation deep into buildings and may be a potential heat source. The heating season is long, but the temperature to be made up is relatively small. There is no significant cooling season as overheating in summer can be accommodated with natural ventilation.

Lessons from the vernacular

Site

Traditionally buildings were usually orientated to minimize the exposure to wind, rather than to encourage solar gains. When choosing the site to build, a sheltered site was preferable to

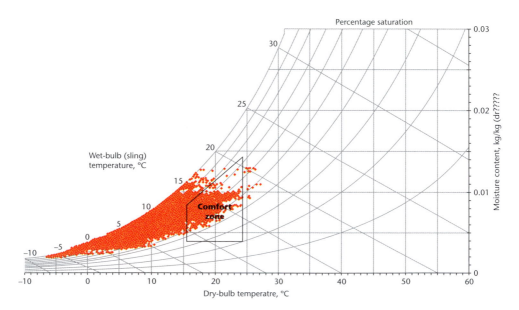

FIGURE 13.1 Psychrometric chart with weather data for Northern Ireland

Source: Meteonorm v5.0

reduce the exposure of the dwelling, but it was also important to build on the least productive piece of land. Often the two came together by building near the base of a sloped site where the gradient of the hill created a shelter belt, and the sloped incline was not a productive piece of land.

Form

A narrow plan evolved due to a lack of timber to span a larger roof plan. The environmental benefits of this narrow plan include cross-ventilation and dual aspects. The dual entry allows for separate access for the inhabitants and the livestock and for cross-ventilation. The most typical plan developed with a hearth in the kitchen at the centre, buffered by the bedroom to one side and byre, which housed the animals, to the other side (see Figures 13.2 and 13.3). The internal organization placed the inhabitants at the warmest point, between the hearth and the livestock, and in the cooler bedroom. The roof is steeply sloped, designed for rain run-off in a climate of high precipitation but where snow rarely lies.

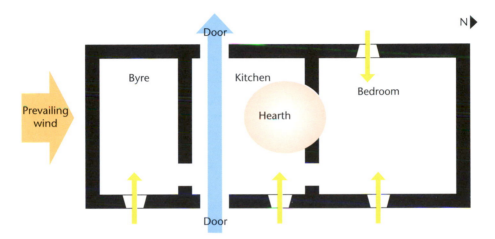

FIGURE 13.2 Typical cottage floor plan showing environmental attributes

FIGURE 13.3 Restored cottage, Co. Donegal, Ireland

Aperture was always on the long walls, catching sun in the morning from the east and in the evening from the west. Small windows reduced heat loss, and the walls around the window were tapered so maximum daylight entered through minimum glazed area. The gable walls incorporated the chimney stack, with the chimney spout at the ridge, protruding through the roof. The dwellings were always extended in length not breadth, through a series of parallel gable walls (Department of environment Northern Ireland, 1994). A farm cottage may require several 'out houses' for the livestock. These were laid out in clusters, often in a courtyard formation, to provide a sheltered outdoor space creating a micro-climate.

Materiality

Building techniques developed with whatever materials the locality provided. The walls of the Irish cottage were traditionally of stone, which provided both the envelope and structure. Stone was cheap and abundant. Walls were constructed either with mortar or by using dry walling techniques, depending on the available local resources. This construction provided a good source of thermal mass to store heat from solar radiation and internal heat gains. In areas that lacked stone, houses were built from peat or mud. Timber was scarce everywhere following the widespread destruction of the forests of Ireland in the sixteenth and seventeenth centuries (Danahar, 1978, pp.9–11).

Mud houses were biodegradable because when no longer in use they would melt back down to the earth. Thatch and mud houses were very comfortable: this building technique provided thermal insulation but low absorption of solar gains, thus providing a warm winter shelter that was cool during the summer. Thatch roofs consisted of a layer of wattle, supporting the top layer of peat from the bog, and a layer of thatch to reduce water penetration in the damp climate. In later years corrugated iron sheeting and slate roofs became increasingly popular as an alternative to thatch.

Space and water heating

There were various styles and sizes of hearths and chimneys used in cottage design, though they were often restricted in size by the 'hearth tax' charged to the residents. Range stoves – installed in place of the open fire – were a later development in rural homes. They provided cooking facilities, hot water and heating for the house and are still popular in rural Irish houses today. Many are now designed for oil fuel but they were originally designed to use solid fuel such as peat or wood.

Design guidelines

The traditional buildings described here evolved in response to their locale and their function on the land, and have several common features. They have a rectangular plan, extending in length, not depth. They are only one room deep, allowing dual aspect daylighting and cross-ventilation. The construction uses thick, strong walls solidly built of mass mineral material supporting a steeply sloped roof. The height is limited to one storey, and designed for protection from the elements rather than for solar gains; the windows and doors are never placed on the gable walls. Finally, an open hearth at floor level in the centre of the plan provides the auxiliary heat source for the house, and heat loss is reduced by buffering either side of this space with a byre and a bedroom.

Design strategies and tools

Design considerations

Space heating accounts for 62 per cent of the annual energy consumption of an average house in the UK and water heating accounts for 22 per cent (Building Research Establishment, 2003). The intention is to reduce the space heating requirement of the scheme and so greatly reduce the overall energy consumption.

Eliminating the need for space heating

A series of tests were performed on a box model using the Energy Index calculation[5] to establish how best to reduce the need for space heating in this climate. The model was of a single-storey detached house with a floor area of 120m² and floor-to-ceiling height of 3m. Four models were tested with variable window-to-floor ratios and with the glazed area concentrated on the south façade to maximize winter solar gains. Model A was based on standard practice insulation levels, with double glazing and curtains (mean window U-value of 2.63 W/m²K). Model B was tested with a double glazing low-emissivity system with night shutters applied from 1900 to 0700 hours and mean window U-value of 1.3 W/m²K. Model C was tested with the same glazing system and improved walls, roof and floor to a mean U-value of 0.1W/m²K for the opaque elements of the building envelope. Finally model D maintained this standard but introduced mechanical ventilation to further reduce the space heating requirement (Figure 13. 4). In all cases the mean whole-house temperature was set at 17°C; this had been determined as the clients' preferred temperature following fieldwork measurements and interviews.

The results show that the optimum window to floor ratio is between 10 per cent and 30 per cent on model D. The double-glazed window with curtains (model A), which is

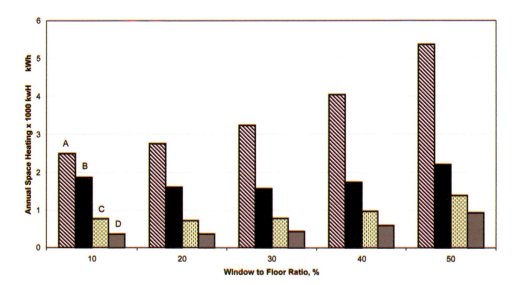

FIGURE 13.4 Effect of window to floor ratio on the annual space heating requirement

commonly preferred in Northern Ireland, increases the annual space heating load proportionately as the area of glazing increases. Although the space heating requirement of the model has been reduced by mechanical ventilation, it has not been eliminated and an auxiliary heat source will have to be specified.

Thermal potential of a sunspace

The design brief includes a sunspace. This provides the opportunity to exploit ambient heat in the environment by collecting and concentrating solar gains in the space and then releasing the pre-warmed air through the rest of the house. Creating this thermal buffer also reduces the heat loss from a highly glazed design. It is a logical expectation that the sunspace will overheat in summer; so shading and ventilation would be employed to counteract this. Reducing the area of glazing would also reduce overheating.

Studies carried out with the Tas simulation model[6] compared thermal performance for model 1 (no sunspace), with model 2 (with attached sunspace) and model 3 (with integrated sunspace) (see Figure 13.5). Each model has the same floor area, window area and construction properties. The sunspaces have a floor area of 24m^2, which is additional to the house floor area of 120m^2, and an aperture of 9m^2 between sunspace and house, 30 per cent of which was assumed to be openable to couple the spaces from 0700 to 1900 hours.

The simulations were performed without a source of auxiliary heat, to predict the internal temperatures of spaces influenced only by climate and internal gains. Results are shown for a sunny day in autumn (Figure 13.6). A maximum difference of 7°C can be clearly seen between the results of the model with integrated sunspace and the model without a sunspace. The predicted temperature of model 3 is some 3°C higher than that of model 2. This is due to the larger exposed surface area of the external sunspace and therefore greater exposure to the elements.

Application in contemporary design

Design brief

As their family are leaving home to pursue careers, the clients have requested a new home that meets their new lifestyle requirements. They now have more time to enjoy as a couple, and their social and work patterns are changing. They require a home with space for their hobbies and have requested a library and an artist's studio. They no longer require the large number of bedrooms they have presently, but request additional sleeping quarters for family visits. It is important that the design considers possible changing future needs and is low maintenance.

Concept design

The form is derived from a synthesis of response to the location, climate and the vernacular. A reclaimed stone 'buffer' wall on the northern boundary protects the house from the cold north wind, reflecting the dense construction of the traditional cottage with minimal aperture (Figure 13.7). This 'buffer' wall is continued inside the plan. Here the wall is entirely an internal thermal mass acting as a spine for the plan, separating and connecting individual spaces,

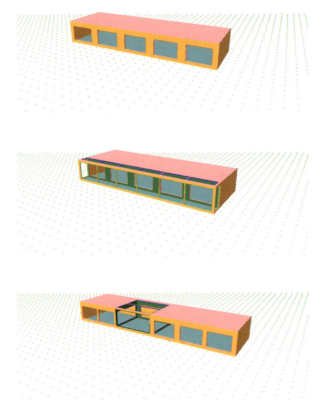

FIGURE 13.5 Tas models used to simulate and assess the performance of a sunspace

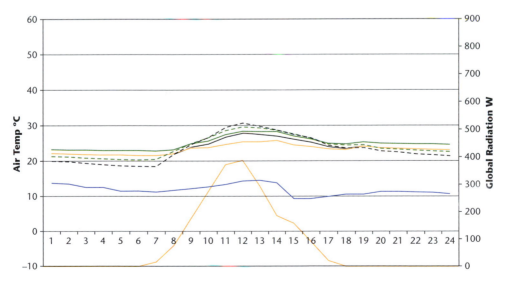

FIGURE 13.6 Thermal performance of the models on a sunny mid-autumn day

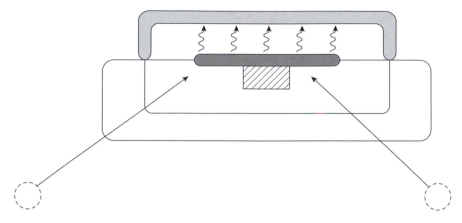

FIGURE 13.7 Concept sketch of building form

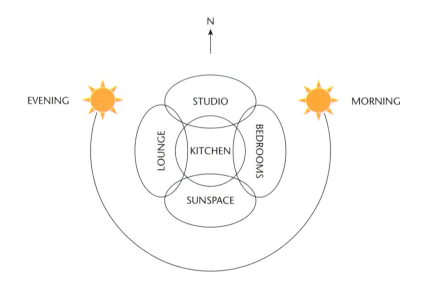

FIGURE 13.8 Concept for internal organization

but also collecting, storing and distributing the heat gains of the internal environment to all spaces in the house. On the south side the building opens up to the sun in a contemporary passive solar design

The organization of this scheme is designed for the daily occupancy of the house to follow the sun path. While the sunspace should face south, the studio requires north light and the kitchen is the warm centre of the house, derived from the vernacular (Figure 13.8).

Form

The intention is for the form to emphasize the contrast between the traditional, dense protective building technique in the north zone, and the open highly glazed south elevation of the passive

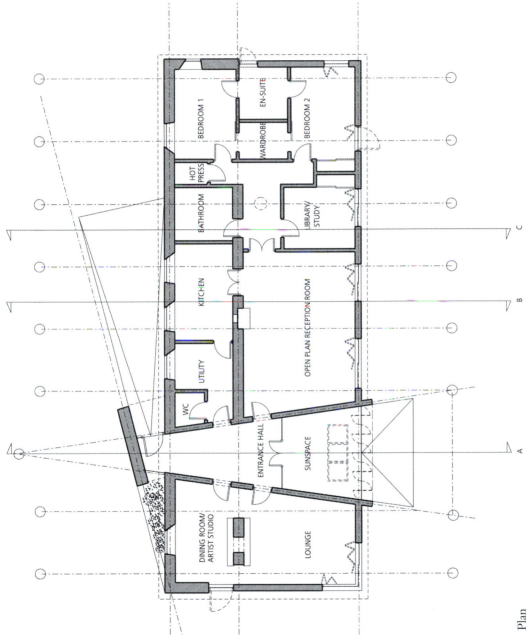

BEDROOM 1

EN-SUITE

WARDROBE

BEDROOM 2

HOT
PRESS

BATHROOM

LIBRARY/
STUDY

KITCHEN

OPEN PLAN RECEPTION ROOM

UTILITY

WC

ENTRANCE HALL

SUNSPACE

DINING ROOM/
ARTIST STUDIO

LOUNGE

A

B

C

FIGURE 13.9 Plan

solar zone. The north zone of the scheme has a massive external stone wall constructed from the reclaimed stone of existing buildings. This is internally insulated for fast thermal response. The south zone is constructed to maximize its passive solar gains, and is insulated externally and with exposed thermal mass in the floor and walls (Figures 13.9 to 13.13).

Orientation

The prevailing wind is a warm mild wind that enters the site from the south. In summer this wind will aid natural ventilation when the aperture, on the south façade, is opened. Glazing is primarily on the south elevation to maximize passive solar gains. Apertures to the north, east and west of the house provide diffuse light, morning sun and views of the sunset respectively. Access is from the north-east of the site, so the entrance is on the north elevation, but facing east to be clearly visible upon arrival; it is also intended that this will shelter the door opening from the cold north winds, and it provides the opportunity to break the dense construction, emphasizing the depth of the stone wall.

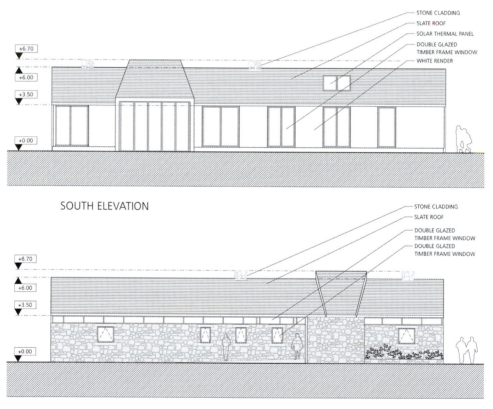

FIGURE 13.10 View of south and north elevations

FIGURE 13.11 View of south and west elevations

FIGURE 13.12 View of north and east elevations

FIGURE 13.13 East elevation showing entrance

Architectural quality

The elongated, single-unit-deep plan of the vernacular is represented in one half of the scheme. To replicate this exactly and meet the requirements of the brief would have created an extremely long, narrow form. Rather, the building is two units deep, yet the overall form retains the proportions of the vernacular, albeit on a slightly larger scale.

The sunspace provides an aspect through the house to the landscape. The studio and library have access to an evening terrace with a south-westerly aspect. The library, hallway and living area all have direct access to the sunspace. The sunspace façade is a folding system, which allows it to become an open, south-facing terrace in summer months. The living area prioritizes the south aspect. The sleeping quarters have developed as a north bedroom for summer occupation and a south bedroom for winter occupation, with an adjoining dressing area allowing easy access from either room. Both bedrooms also open onto a morning terrace with a south-easterly aspect.

Glazing system

Shutters reduce window heat loss at night without affecting solar gains in daylight hours. In this scheme the shutters are fitted internally for easy access in winter evenings. Inside they are less prone to weathering, and therefore require less maintenance. The shutters can be left open in summer months when night cooling of the space would provide a better environment for the following day.

The smaller windows in the stone buffer wall replicate the characteristics of the vernacular window; the inner walls are tapered to maximize daylight penetration while minimizing heat loss. A large roof overhang on the south elevation will protect the façade from weathering by reducing exposure to the sun, rain and snow. The depth of overhang prevents passive solar gains in summer, without reducing passive solar gains in winter. The glazing system specified is low emissivity double glazing with a U-value of $1.8W/m^2K$ reduced to $0.8W/m^2K$ with night shutters closed. Assuming the shutters are closed from 1900 to 0700 hours, the mean 24-hour U-value of the glazing will be $1.3W/m^2K$.

Ventilation

Providing ample aperture at both high and low levels encourages natural ventilation. The air warmed in the sunspace is used for ventilation and reduces the need for space heating in the dwelling. A façade designed to open completely converts the sunspace into a roofed courtyard in summer (Figures 13.14 and 13.15).

Alternative roofing system

The detailing of the junction between the roof and the gable wall is derived from the vernacular. The south pitch has a series of 1m² modules, including south-facing glazing panels, solar collectors and photovoltaic panels. These modules actively and passively generate energy for the house and are incorporated into the design as a considered element in the form.

Autonomous architecture

The houses of rural Northern Ireland are not connected to mains sewage systems or fuel source. They may connect to the mains water supply and national grid. Fuel for heating systems must be stored on site; currently oil is the most popular fuel. Many rural homes have wells and use this as their water supply (Figure 13.16).

FIGURE 13.14 Section through sunspace

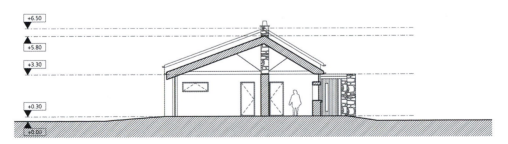

FIGURE 13.15 Section through kitchen and lounge

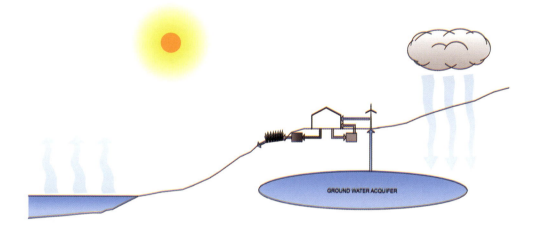

FIGURE 13.16 Proposed water system

As the internal gains will not meet all the heating requirements, the clients have specified a traditional range stove to provide the cooking facilities for the house. These stoves provide a continuous source of background heat, auxiliary heating and hot water. The solid fuel stoves can run on wood, smokeless fuel or peat. The stove outputs a constant 0.5kW which increases to 1.0kW when in use for cooking.[7] In winter this background heat often brings the internal environment of the living space up to the preferred thermal comfort levels without additional heating. As the studio and library may not be occupied at all times, additional heating required for these spaces may be generated only when required. The internal 'heat distribution' wall connects the living space to the winter, south-facing bedroom and provides thermal mass to retain the heat of the house.

The clients have always lived in this cool temperate climate and are robust and well adjusted. Dataloggers were used to monitor their thermal comfort levels in their current residence. A week of testing concluded that their preferred whole house temperature is 18°C. However, this is expected to rise to 21°C when they become elderly. The thermal performance of the scheme was simulated in Tas with a mean whole house temperature of 18°C. The graph shows the annual energy consumption of the clients' current house compared to the new proposal with and without the range stove. The results show the range stove is not the most efficient heat source, as the energy of the continuous heat supply is greater than the actual required energy (Figure 13.17).

Conclusion

Lessons from the vernacular combined with contemporary design techniques have been the driving forces throughout the design process with the goal of incorporating appropriate form,

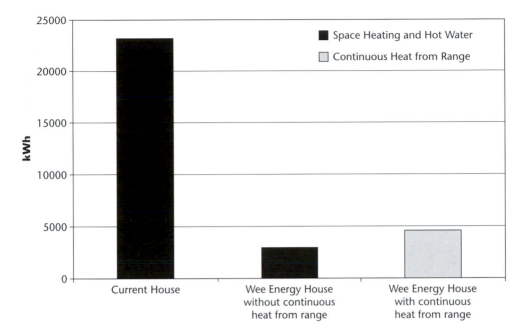

FIGURE 13.17 The predicted annual energy requirement for space heating

organization and materials to create a house that reflects the age we live in. The final scheme is simple, energy-efficient, contemporary architecture for rural Northern Ireland. It is designed to keep running costs and maintenance low with regard to the stringent planning regulations for the countryside. The techniques of using south-facing glazing for passive solar gains and the incorporation of a sunspace, coupled with high insulation and natural ventilation, greatly enhance the thermal performance of the house without increasing the budget, because the architecture becomes the technology in this design. The reduction of energy consumption will greatly reduce the carbon emissions of the house and hence its overall impact on the global environment. The water management system, reclamation of materials and mini-mization of construction waste will reduce the building's effect on the local environment. The advantages of this design include contemporary self-sufficient design, reduced energy requirements and a strong aesthetic link to the vernacular that enhances the countryside of Northern Ireland.

Notes

1   Northern Ireland Census, 2001.
2   Meteotest, Meteonorm v.5.2, 2004, Global Meteorological Database for Solar Energy and Applied Climatology.
3   Met Eiranne, Irish Meteorological Office, 2003.
4   A. Fleming, interview, Northern Ireland, 2004.
5   S. Yannas, Energy Index, Sustainable Environmental Studies Programme, Architectural Association Graduate School, London, 1994–2000.
6   Environmental Design Solutions Limited, Tas New Generation Software.
7   G. Brown, engineer and technical advisor for Rayburn Range Stoves, 2005.

References

Building Research Establishment (2003) *Domestic Energy Factfile*, London, BRE Bookshop-Publishers.

Danahar, K. (1978) *Ireland's Vernacular Architecture*, Cork, The Mercier Press.

Department of Environment Northern Ireland (1994) *Design Guide for Rural Northern Ireland*, Belfast, DOE.

14

THE VERNACULAR AS A MODEL FOR SUSTAINABLE DESIGN

Wayne Forster, Amanda Heal and Caroline Paradise

Introduction

Considering the quantity and diversity of vernacular architecture in the world, it plays a surprisingly small part in architectural education. Where academics do address vernacular architecture, it usually involves historic documentation. The 'Vernacular Architecture in the Twenty-First Century: Theory Education and Practice' conference aimed:

> to further the debate on the importance of ver-
> nacular architecture studies now and throughout
> the twenty-first century, not as a study of past
> traditions, but as a contribution to new methods,
> solutions and achievements for the future built
> environment.
>
> (Asquith and Vellinga, 2006, p.xv)

This paper describes an innovative educational method that uses vernacular buildings as a source for teaching sustainable design.

Today, sustainable design and building technology are fundamental to the education of architectural students. With the ever-growing global concern for the use of energy and resources and associated climate change, architects have a greater responsibility to design buildings that are environmentally sustainable. The performance of these buildings must also ensure a comfortable and healthy atmosphere for their occupants. It is therefore important that architecture students develop a thorough understanding of climate, building performance

MAP 14 Cardiff, Wales, UK

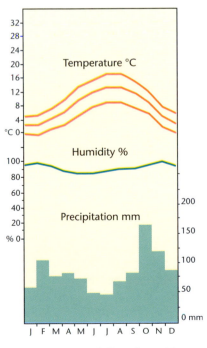

GRAPH 14 Cardiff, Wales, UK

and human comfort at an early stage in their education. Indeed, the RIBA's *Tomorrow's architect* states: 'at Part 1 students will demonstrate [. . .] the ability to integrate knowledge of human well being, the welfare of future generations, the natural world, consideration of a sustainable environment [and] use of materials'. (RIBA, 2003)

Recently, there has been a reliance on energy-consuming technology in the form of heating, cooling, ventilation and lighting systems to achieve human comfort in buildings. These systems are often 'added on' once the form, layout and materiality of the building have been decided. An approach to design where building technology is integrated with concept design has the potential to reduce the need for high-tech systems and reduce the energy consumption of buildings.

In most schools of architecture, issues of building technology, sustainability and environmental performance are taught in the lecture theatre. The problem with this method of teaching is that the lecture theatre is detached both from the design studio and from real buildings and their surroundings. Building technology modules are often a series of theoretical lessons on individual topics, followed by lessons in how these might be applied to design. Students then find it difficult to understand how to integrate these lessons with their design concepts, and technology becomes an element to add in the later stages of a design project in order to meet course requirements. Furthermore, the lecture theatre environment does nothing to make this an engaging and stimulating subject. Many students find it a boring necessity, and its important relevance to architectural design is lost.

Aims of the World Architecture module

The World Architecture module is taught to undergraduate students at the Welsh School of Architecture during their first semester at the school. The module employs real vernacular buildings in context as practical, experience-based learning environments. Studies are undertaken by the students with the aim of developing an in-depth and ingrained knowledge of the complex ways in which buildings interact with the environment. It is hoped that students' understanding will become intuitive through these experiences early in their education, and that they will see building technology not as a set of isolated scientific principles but as an essential and integral part of projects from the concept design stage.

Vernacular buildings make good models for sustainable design lessons and are used as 'laboratories' by students during the module. They are comprehensible due to their often simple forms and resourceful use of materials and technology, meaning that lessons can be easily demonstrated and then adopted by students in their design work.

Vernacular architecture tends to respond to climatic conditions using passive, low-energy strategies to provide for human comfort – strategies that are integral to the form, orientation and materiality of the buildings. This architecture also demonstrates an economical use of local building resources and is, therefore, an ideal resource for teaching sustainable design.

Module outline

St Fagans Week

A key part of the World Architecture module involves students in an intensive, week-long block course at the St Fagans Museum of Welsh Life near Cardiff. St Fagans is an open-air museum that displays a variety of real vernacular buildings that have been moved from locations throughout Wales. These 'exhibits' are set in context within the extensive grounds of the museum and re-erected 'stone by stone' as they were in their original location. There are over forty examples, ranging from cottages and farmhouses to a school, chapel, barns, pigsty and a tannery, which represent various periods in Welsh history (Figure 14.1). Each exhibit is 'displayed' to give a sense of how people would have lived or worked in the building in the past.

During the block week, students learn about a number of building technology themes: Site and Climate, Structure and Materials, Thermal Environment, Visual Environment and Acoustic Environment. Each day of the course begins with in-situ talks and demonstrations by subject specialists from the school, using the buildings and their contexts to explain the principles of the theme and how it can be observed, measured and analysed (Figure 14.2).

Following the demonstrations, in small groups the students observe, measure and analyse the theme in one of the domestic building exhibits, considering its relationship to culture and the lives of the occupants. They individually record and explain the information gathered through sketches and annotations in a notebook, developing essential architectural skills (Figures 14.3–14.6).

Lecture series

The block course is accompanied by a series of World Architecture lectures that use examples of vernacular architecture from around the globe to illustrate further building design topics and to give an insight into other vernacular cultures. Issues such as Culture, Function and

FIGURE 14.1 Abernodwydd Farmhouse, St Fagans

FIGURE 14.2 In-situ demonstration by subject specialist

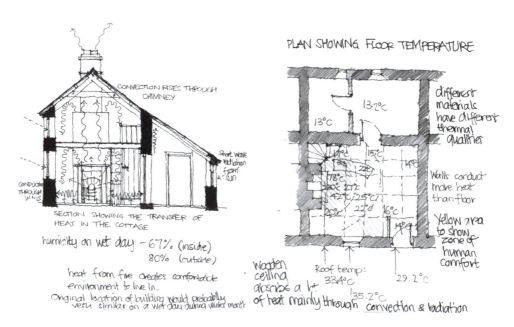

FIGURE 14.3 Notebook example: thermal environment

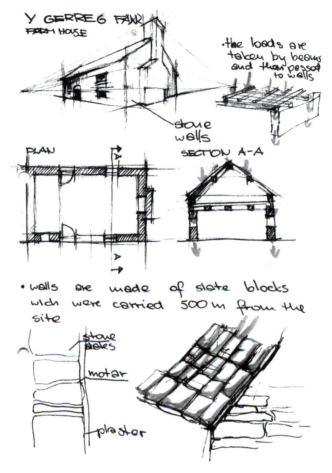

FIGURE 14.4 Notebook example: structure and materials

Use, Gravity and Wind, Materials, Settlement and Refinement help to tie together building technology with other aspects of design through studies in the vernacular. Students are set weekly, lecture-related studies that add to their notebooks.

'Model' and Design Week

The module culminates in a week-long design exercise that aims to put students' new skills and knowledge into practice. First, they are asked to develop and draw a 'model' based on their understanding of vernacular architecture. Using their model, they then design a small building, such as an artist's or writer's hut, that they must site in a given location.

Course outcomes

Through learning in real buildings rather than in the lecture theatre, students are able to experience the climatic conditions and internal environments they are studying. As well as gaining knowledge of the scientific principles, they can see, smell, hear and feel the

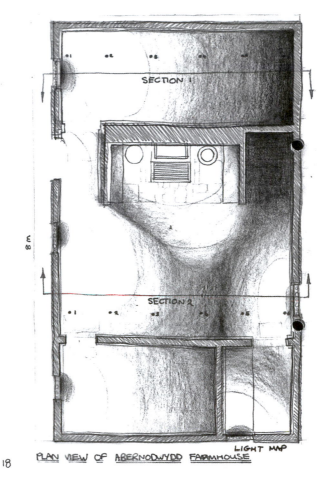

FIGURE 14.5 Notebook example: visual environment

architecture, developing a sensory awareness of its physical characteristics: What does 300 lux feel like? How warm does it have to be to feel comfortable in this space? These are the sorts of questions that students can find answers to through this learning method (Figure 14.7). The museum setting also encourages students to imagine how people would have interacted with the buildings and, therefore, how the buildings provided for their needs. This deeper understanding means that they can start to intuitively make design decisions that use the building to modify the climate in a resourceful and responsible way.

Using the vernacular buildings at St Fagans gives students a holistic understanding of the built environment. The buildings simply demonstrate how climate can be modified through orientation, form, materiality and layout to achieve conditions for human comfort internally. (They also highlight that perception of human comfort has changed through history, and this makes students review their own perceptions of comfort.) Vernacular architecture does not rely on high-tech, energy-consuming systems for heating, cooling, ventilation and lighting, and it therefore encourages students to think about passive, sustainable systems in their own designs. To adopt passive environmental systems requires consideration in the early stages of

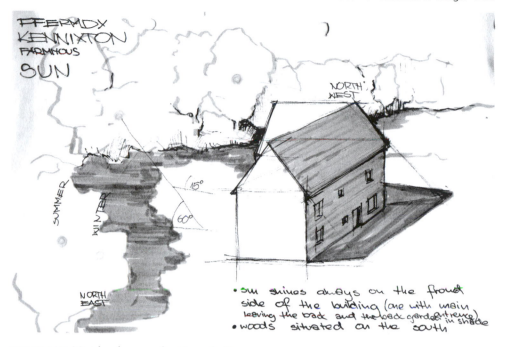

FFERMDX
KENNIXTON
FARMHOUS
SUN

NORTH WEST

SUMMER
WINTER
15°
60°

NORTH EAST

• sun shines always on the front side of the building (one with main leaving the back and the back garden/entrence) in shade
• woods situated on the south

FIGURE 14.6 Notebook example: site and climate

FIGURE 14.7 Students learn through tactile experience

design, when initial decisions about orientation, form and materiality are being made. The World Architecture module stresses the links between building technology, sustainability and concept design. Through their studies at St Fagans, students understand how site and climate, built form and people are integrated through design (Figure 14.8).

As well as providing a wealth of knowledge, the intensive block–course allows students to quickly develop a range of practical architectural skills. These skills, such as site measuring, observing, analysing and sketching, are valuable to students for the rest of their studies and future careers.

The week-long design exercise that concludes the World Architecture module is a chance for students to put into practice their new skills and understanding. In developing a 'model' for design that is informed by issues of vernacular architecture, they are compelled to consider how the lessons they have learnt are relevant to design right from the concept stage. They re-examine their understanding of response to site and climate, use of materials and resources, structure and construction and building form and use. Their design decisions are based on observations and experience of real buildings, producing considered and realistic outcomes to add to their design portfolios.

The vernacular as a model

The use of the vernacular as a model is in line with current thinking on vernacular architecture. At the 'Vernacular Architecture in the Twenty-First Century: Theory Education and Practice' conference in December 2005, Amos Rapoport presented his paper 'Vernacular design as a model system'. He suggests that it is time that vernacular studies moved on from 'describing and documenting buildings' to 'the next "problem-oriented", comparative,

FIGURE 14.8 Site, building form and people are integrated

integrative and more conceptual/theoretical stage': that we should learn from vernacular design, and that 'this is best done by looking at vernacular design as a *model system*' (Rapoport, 2006, pp.179–180). He argues that this approach bridges the gap between real buildings and theory.

Rapoport discourages the copying of 'certain formal qualities (shapes, massing, details etc.), often based on a romanticised version of the vernacular', but suggests that a more 'valid approach is to derive more or less general lessons and principles by analysing vernacular environments using [. . .] models and the like, and applying these lessons to design' (Rapoport, 2006, p.182).

Among other topics, he identifies that vernacular buildings can offer lessons in response to climate, energy use and notions of environmental quality; and that vernacular design can 'offer a most useful entry point' to these studies because aspects are more 'clear-cut, more extreme, [. . .] rather than the more ambiguous cases of many present day environments' (Rapoport, 2006, p.183).

Rapoport's paper, as well as others presented at the conference, emphasize the potential contribution that studies in the vernacular can make to the education of the architects of the future.

Conclusion

The World Architecture module at the Welsh School of Architecture employs the collection of vernacular buildings at St Fagans to address the challenges faced in teaching sustainable design. It makes building technology an engaging and stimulating subject for students at an early stage in their education, stressing its importance in a holistic approach to design.

The studies undertaken provide students with an integrated understanding of site and climate, sustainable building design and human well-being. The experiential methods of teaching and learning lead to an embedded awareness of the issues related to this subject, allowing students to intuitively apply lessons learned to their design work. During the course the students quickly develop a range of skills and techniques that will be valuable to their studies and as architects of the future.

Other schools of architecture could benefit by drawing on vernacular architecture as a source of information and inspiration. In this way, more students could be taught sustainability and building technology as an integrated part of the design process.

This paper has identified one way in which vernacular architecture can contribute to the future of the built environment, through education, as a model for sustainable design.

Acknowledgements

The work of the following students illustrates this paper: Oliver Forsyth, Kaja Delezuch and Simon Broomfield.

References

Asquith, L. and Vellinga, M., 2006, *Vernacular Architecture in the Twenty-first Century: Theory, Education and Practice*, London, Taylor & Francis.

Rapoport, A., 2006, 'Vernacular design as a model system', in L. Asquith and M. Vellinga (eds) *Vernacular architecture in the twenty-first century: theory education and practice*, London, Taylor & Francis.

RIBA, 2003, *Tomorrow's Architect*, London, RIBA.

INDEX